It Rings True
Guidance from
The Council

A Channeled Book
By Ron Head

Editing and final compilation by Annette Despain

ISBN 13: 978-1523385546

ISBN 10: 1523385545

Also by Ron Head:

The Wisdom of Michael: Messages from an Archangel

Acknowledgments

Annette Despain has put much effort into the compilation and editing of these messages. I also would like to thank the following people, all of whom I consider good friends, without whom this book would never have been written. First came April Colon who taught me ThetaHealing® and began my journey into the world of expanded consciousness. Suzanne Spooner taught me her TAUK method and thus started my opening to becoming a channel. Next came Dolores Cannon, now in spirit, whose teachings of Quantum Healing Hypnosis Therapy have led me into further explorations of reality. Paul Selig and his guides have put me on a journey which I trust will never come to an end. Thank you each for all you have contributed.

Foreword

We are living in monumental times of great change upon our planet and within the hearts and consciousness of humanity. For each person on Earth, it is a time of spiritual awakening; a remembrance of soul identity and purpose, an integration of all aspects of one's being; physical, mental, emotional and spiritual. This awakening is being felt and manifested on all levels of life on Earth, and everything is being transformed in this process, including the healing arts, with greater emphasis now on healing the whole person through natural and holistic modalities; embodying a spirituality which goes beyond former boundaries of religious creeds and belief systems, greater environmental awareness and sensitivity, with many people choosing alternative life-styles, and an increasing awareness of other dimensions of existence which comes as they attune to the cosmos and increase their light quotient which is another way of saying, their consciousness.

One has only to read or listen to the daily news to be apprised of the minute-by-minute changes which are taking place within the systems that have served humanity and the greater good of all. Those systems are now collapsing and transforming into ones which will *truly* serve the highest good for all so that everyone upon the planet can expand and embrace a more enlightened perspective of the process of evolution that is now rapidly taking place.

Ron Head's latest book is filled with gentle and oftentimes humorous reminders for those who have or are in the process now of awakening to their own spiritual journey and realizing their unique and important place in the eternal scheme of the cosmos. It contains many gems of wisdom, timely insights and guidance that is most helpful, practical and heart warming.

May you enjoy this book as much as I have! May its Light shine ever more brightly as its message spreads across the planet!

Marlene Swetlishoff, Scribe/Channel for Ascended Master Hilarion and the Ascended Realms of Light. Author of, "The Hilarion Connection©, Book One".

Introduction

As described in the introduction to the prior book, The Wisdom of Michael, I began channeling Archangel Michael after learning ThetaHealing® and Suzanne Spooner's TAUK method. As I practiced this daily over the months, the actual procedure continued to modify, seemingly on its own. I relied less and less upon the mechanics I had learned and more on the feeling of the connection itself. I have since come to understand from others that this is normal.

In April of 2013, Suzanne came to Florida with her husband, a pilot, for an air show. I met them in St. Petersburg, and Suzanne gave me my first session of Dolores Cannon's regression hypnosis. It was a life changing event. I subsequently moved to Des Moines, Iowa so that Suzanne and I could continue these sessions, and we became close friends.

I believe that the opening of my consciousness that resulted from my having many hypnosis sessions resulted in a steadily increasing clarity and purpose for my channeling. It certainly felt and continues to feel that way.

At this point in the progression of my channeling, the messages began to be delivered by 'Michael for The Council'. More and more often the messengers would just identify themselves as The

Council. But I continued to associate AA Michael with them.

I knew, from several comments, that quite a few readers felt a connection to him, and I was reluctant to drop the name. I also knew that the archangels were a part of the Councils, so I didn't think it would be a problem. But apparently, the Council had other ideas. The time between messages got longer and longer. When I finally got the hint and began identifying the source as The Council, they resumed their frequency, and as you will see, they very much want us to know how things work and how they fit into the scheme of things. They have gone to quite some lengths to explain this to us as the first section of this book will show.

As before, I have been immensely helped in compiling and editing this text by my good friend, Annette Despain. We hope you like the result as much as we do.

Table of Contents

The Council   1

Who are The Council and what is its purpose?

Change   19

Exploring the mechanics of change

Power   41

The power of our individual selves

Light and Energy   57

Because it's everything

Self-love and Worthiness   77

Two of the most important topics of ascension

Your Divine Nature   83

What we must remember about ourselves

Consciousness   99

And everything is conscious

Purpose and Path   105

Why are we here and where are we going?

Forgiveness 117

Another must

Freedom and Free Will 123

Is it real?

The Flow 133

What is it and how do I get into it?

What Is Happening 139

Another viewpoint

Miscellaneous 167

Safety, Gratitude, Discernment, Abundance/Response Ability, Positivity, Value

Ascension 183

What all the rest was about

The Council

Let us begin these messages for your year of 2014 with a new understanding of where this information will be coming from. Nothing will, in fact, have changed, but we want to make it clearer to each of you where this guidance originates.

As you see above, I am speaking now for what we will call the Councils. Some channels call these groups, some call it other things. But no matter what its name, it is the fact that each of you has, and in fact participates in, councils who guide you and every other sentient being on this journey. You visit these councils. Your Higher Selves sit here. Your guides and your angels do, as well.

From where you sit at this moment, all the way up to the very highest consciousness in these universes, there are participants guiding all of us forward. As we move through this year, we wish to make it more and more comfortable for you to understand and feel that these messages are not coming from some source to which you have no access. Rather, they come from that within each of you to which you have total access and always have had.

Our goal, always, is to make this more and more common for each of you to participate in and to know that you have always taken part in. We want you to feel at home with this process so that it becomes easier and easier for you. The energies of which most channels have spoken so very often have now lifted your collective consciousness high enough to make this a very viable possibility for you this year, if you so desire.

So you will, from today, see these messages delivered by myself, by others who wish to step forward, or simply headed "The Council". Whatever the name in the heading, please understand that you have taken part in this entire process. And since that is so, understand also that you are our dear friends and family.

As we have told you so often, you are never alone. We know every dream, every thought, and every prayer just as intimately as do you, and we begin working on them as soon as you make them.

We will also be reminding you, from time to time, of ways to smooth that path, so to speak. But you very likely have reached understandings that will require only reminders. So let us make this new year we are embarking on a very abundant and magical year for each of you.

We are here today to bring you another look at the subject we brought up in an earlier message. That subject is the make-up of who you are, of who we are.

This seems to be a very complex and difficult subject from your point of view, but we assure you that it is not. The difficulty lies only in the newness of the thought for you. And then, of course, there are those who cannot or will not entertain such thoughts for their own personal reasons.

Most of you who are reading this are those for whom that does not apply. It is time for you to begin to understand that you are a great deal more than what is surrounded by your physical bodies. Also, consider that this applies to every other person and every other entity around you. Even though your senses tell you that you have limits, that you are separate from everything, it is not, in fact, true. But that will lead us off on another tangent.

What we wish to dispel now is your perception that life happens to you. And while we are at it, let's also get rid of the thought that things are determined before you get 'here', and there is nothing you can do about it. There is no conflict between the ideas of councils guiding your life and the fact that you are a being of free will.

Now, why is that? Dearest friends, that is because just beyond the veil of your forgetting, there is a continuance of you that sits with us and receives this guidance and agrees with it, in fact, helps to formulate it. You, in great part, are guiding you. And yet, even when you entertain this idea, you say, "I would never choose this!"

You say that in your moments of pain, and we tell you that you would, and you did. The trick, if it is one at all, is to look beyond the painful and ask, "In what way is this serving me?" That is a **very** difficult question to fathom in many situations. We do understand that. But it is true, nevertheless.

There is no being in this entire universe, or indeed, any other, who decides to make you suffer for anything. Well, with the exception of yourself, of course. We ask you to look at this possibility. When and if life is not as you would have it be, where and for what are you judging yourself as less than, as wrong, as guilty, as needing to make up for? And if you just cannot imagine what that might be, that is all right. Forgive yourself anyway. For what might you be unable to forgive self when your Creator has already forgiven you? Are you really that harsh on yourself? Well, yes, you are, dear friends. In many, many cases, you are indeed.

And you are separated from us and from Creator? It is not possible for you to be separate from Creator. You live in that illusion. You are never held separate from us or your guides or your families here, either. There is, here, a much larger portion of you than you can imagine who is never apart from us. And so, in order to deal with your life, you have created another illusion.

And then there is the truth that, were you able to perceive the truth of all we have just explained, you would not wish to remain where you are. And where you are right now is very much where you wished to be at this time.

Take heart dear ones. We know that it is a difficult place you find yourselves in. But you are there right now in order to change that and also to witness and experience that change. The heavy lifting is almost all completely done now. You are now in the position of learning how to bring about that which you desire with far less opposition than heretofore. The biggest problem for you now will be that change is often messy. But, as it will also be unfolding and not sudden, there will also be much to celebrate and delight in.

Returning to the initial subject of this message, you will very soon begin, in fact many of you have already begun, to feel the understanding of your Greater Selves and their relationship with the All. This will be something that will grow in you over all of your existence, but it begins. Thank you for your attention throughout this rather lengthy message. Love to you all, dear friends. Good day.

Our topic for discussion today is The Councils. All of you have experience of these. Many of you have memories and dreams of this. Even the very best efforts to describe these to you will fall very far short, but you have reached a level of awareness now that makes it possible to begin acquainting your conscious minds with this image, this interpretation of 'how things work'.

More and more of you, in your remembrance of dreams or meditations, are seeing what you variously call auditoriums, amphitheaters, or council chambers. Most are seeing these as of immense size and participation. This is, in actuality, a representation you have constructed to allow understanding of an energetic event that you have witnessed. Such things must be 'seen' by you in this way in order to understand the events you participate in.

When you are 'there', in that 'place', you 'see' a meeting being conducted in which you participate in decisions that affect you. The reason for the quotation marks in the prior sentence is that everything we are describing is an internal experience within your being. That really is unimportant at this point. There will come a time when you experience the truth of that. In the meantime, we will describe such things in the linear fashion which you currently experience.

Many report seeing great numbers of beings in these councils. They see some that appear to be in body and many more whom they sense as being spirit or light beings. They see guides, teachers, and angelic beings. Sometimes they witness themselves as listening and other times as speaking. All of this is true.

What we wish you to begin to consider and to understand is that these councils are where all decisions that affect you in any way are being made. You are always there. And no decision is ever made without your express consent. Usually, it is you who is asking for all of the information you need to make a decision regarding a proposed life course. This is where you have decided to experience all that has happened in your lives, including the current one, and where you continue to do so. All decisions made in these councils are made in unanimity. You might think, "What if there is disagreement?" That is not the way on these planes. When the entirety of future consequence is known, the choice will always be toward what is best for yourself and for all.

The attendance is made up of all those who are able to contribute in any way toward your knowledge and understanding. Nothing has ever been decided and acted upon without your complete agreement. And most importantly, please contemplate that, as there is really no such thing as linear time, you are currently participating in those decisions and living out the results at the same time. As a matter of fact, all of the other facets of your Self are in that meeting, as well. Your guides are all there. Your teachers are there. It is amazing to see. All of you are creating an even greater life than you imagine. And all of you are contributing your knowledge and experience to the whole.

Think what a magnificent being it must take to create such a miraculous thing as the life you are leading, fitting it neatly and expertly into the workings of the infinite so that the highest and best interests of all are considered. As you like to say, you rock!

We will speak again soon. We have allowed some quiet time for you and for this channel to work with and assimilate the changes of the just passed cosmic alignments. We will settle back into our normal conversations with you now. Good day.

It is a time of new beginnings. The channel has begun a new chapter in his life, and we will begin developing a line of information that it is now time for you to understand.

We began months ago heading these messages 'Michael and the Councils'. It seemed that too few were able to maintain interest unless the name of an Archangel was attached to the message. We believe that now you have progressed in your understanding enough for you to be told that all of the messages originate in a level of consciousness that includes your guides, the masters, as you call them, angels, teachers, light beings, and the most divine ones whom you all revere. We will now call ourselves The Council.

Understand that each of you has a council. Each of you sits on a council. As we have spoken before, your council is always in session, and all decisions are unanimous. Nothing is ever decided upon that will affect you and which you have not agreed to. As much as it may seem that way to you from your human perspective, it is just not so. The YOU that has agreed to, and, in fact, has probably asked for, the experiences in your life, has a far greater understanding and goal in mind than you can fathom with your current level of consciousness. That is about to change, however. In fact, as we have also said before, that is changing now. The growth much of humanity is going through is now becoming quite evident, even though it is, by your reckoning, gradual and subtle.

The object of these messages is, and always has been, to aid you in your growth and help you to remember knowledge which you all carry but have forgotten how to access. This challenge is being addressed in many other ways, as well. Many of your healers are learning to lead you past your personal blockages, to heal your wounds and tear down your inner walls. Much of the problem has been your inability to stop judging yourselves and those you see around you. And there are other things in your way, also. We shall address these as we come to them.

It is time. You have come to what may be termed a crossroads. The time has come for plain talk and for focus on the most important things. We are sorry, but much of what you 'get' is just not a priority in the overall picture. We understand that you are living in places where things seem to be important that will be understood later to be less so. We understand that it is not possible for one to concentrate on lofty matters when one is hungry or in great danger. But most of you are not truly in those types of situations. And in fact, you would be amazed to know how many of those who are in them address us more often than many of you do.

So the point of today's message is that we, as The Council, will now begin addressing questions centered more on aiding you in your quest for greater access to your own higher consciousness. We will not be instructing you in how to meditate, although we will urge you to do so. We will not be espousing any particular beliefs, although we urge you to closely examine them. But we want you to find out who and what you are. And we know that now is the time for you to do that.

Now, if it helps you to think of us in terms of Universal Mind, Buddha Mind, Oversoul, or any other thing you wish to call us, please feel free to do so. We do not care. All of these terms being coined by your human minds are necessarily limited by your understandings and are, therefore, less than accurate. Even 'The Council' is limiting, but we understand that some name must be chosen. The important piece of information for you to receive today is that the consciousness that we speak from is within you. It is within each one of you. We can be reached by each of you. And in fact, if you all did that, we would have no need at all for these channelings. But there are many levels of awakening, and each must begin where he or she stands.

Good day for now. We will continue soon and much more often. There is much to speak about.

We will speak today of an increasingly frequent experience that you, or a great many of you, are having in dreams, lucid dreams, meditations, out-of-body experiences, and waking visions. We know it is also spoken of increasingly in channeled messages from many of us. We refer to what you are calling board meetings, council meetings, meetings on star ships, etc.

What is going on here, and why are so many reporting it? Why is it described in so many different ways?

You are finding yourselves experiencing yourselves in a new and expanded way. You are meeting masters, teachers, guides, light beings, angels. You remember in detail or quite vaguely. But you know something very important happened. We would inform you of several things for you to ponder upon.

These meetings have always been a part of your reality. They are how you plan your lives. What is new to you is that you are becoming conscious of the fact. The beings that you are meeting are actually known to you from your infinite past, or would be if there were such a thing as the past. Let's not go there. And the differing settings and descriptions are merely your conscious mind's attempt to make sense in your experience of what you perceived in a quite different and entirely energetic plane.

Now, why is this happening now? You are going to discover many things as this continues and as your life begins to change. Most importantly, you are going to find out who you are and what you are. Why are you here? This has always been your 'searing, burning question', has it not? Well, you are going to answer it for yourselves.

This has also been the purpose, always, of these messages, no matter the stated source. It will continue to be. You call us masters, guides, and angels. What are we masters of? Where do we guide you to? What are we messengers of? What other types of messages are as important?

Often you speak of the 'veil'. What does the veil separate you from if not this knowledge? Well, the veil is becoming thinner and thinner now. In fact, it is positively tattered and torn. And the experiences we have been describing are your new glimpses of what you've seen on the other side of it.

One other note we would add. As you have more of these experiences, claim them as an integral part of your lives. These are your councils, your assemblies. You have a place upon them, a place which you have a right to. You exist in service to them, and please believe us, they exist in service to you, as well.

These things are our ongoing message to you and one which we shall not vary from until it is known by you as a part of your very being. You have no need any longer for believing yourselves to be less than you are. And there is a great need for you to be all that you are.

With the greatest blessings of love and light, we wish you good day.

Today, let us discuss this assembly further. Let us explore the reason for and the make-up of what we are calling this Council.

Many of you, as we have previously mentioned, have had dreams, visions, or meditations in which you have seen yourselves watching or speaking before a meeting of a council. Some have seen a board meeting, an auditorium, a stadium, etc. We have spoken of that, as well. We shall, in future, assure that this is the experience of many more of you. It is not that you have not been

a part of such, you see, but that you do not
remember it upon awakening. Ask for that to be
remedied, if you wish.

The experience is very similar, but not
identical, for all; however, some are able to accept
more accurate recall than are others. Let us assure
you that the truth of the Council is that for each of
you, there is available, at all times, every bit of
information and guidance that you require in your
present lifetime. That means, in your terms, that
this body consists of guides, angels, light beings for
which you have no other name, loved ones,
teachers, what we have named teachers of
teachers, any source of guidance and loving care
and aid that you could possible need. Your own
Highest Self is always in attendance.

We have said also that your council never
adjourns. It has always been in session, and it
always will be. Its members will vary as your needs
vary. Frequently, other versions of you will be in
attendance.

Now let us examine the why of all that. You
have chosen to experience a life that does not, as it
is currently being lived, have the normal
completeness of your memory and consciousness
in body. A great deal of your purpose, especially in
the life you are currently focused upon, is to
complete the ascension of those bodies, and we are
speaking of your collective, into a state in which

that is no longer the case. And here is the important core of this message. You are not, and never were, intended to do this monumental thing without help. Although it may seem to be the case, it is not happening in that way.

So instead of continuing to experience that condition throughout your life, which you may do if you choose, we recommend that you make every effort possible to allow yourself to experience and believe otherwise. Your acceptance is required, you see. It is the belief in a separation that holds the veil in place. You have been taught that as a fact for a very long time, and you have learned the lesson well. We are not separate from you, not in time, not in place, not in any way. So begin, we suggest, by simply allowing for the possibility.

This will eventually begin to bring, in one way or another, the possibility that you are, indeed, a divine being into your awareness. Now, where you are, that may seem a huge thing to accept. So we have another suggestion for you. Seek out those who embody characteristics that you admire. See the divine in them. Use this mirror that we spoke to you of in another message. Then realize that they are not different from you. They are aspects of the One expressing in the world, for the world, and so are you. So are you.

We have not been in the practice of doling out instruction. And it appears to some that we are increasingly doing just that. But, dear, dear friends, the time is approaching when everything that you are will be needed. You will need to believe in yourselves as never before. And the well from which you may draw is available to you even now. The water is love. It is light. It is divine knowing. Why wait?

It Rings True

Change

We bear a message today regarding the speeding up of the manifestation of those concrete changes on your planet for which you have been waiting so long. There is, at last, an over-balance reached that allows your intents, those of the ones you term lightworkers, to override more of the negative that still remains. Therefore, you will see, or are seeing, an almost daily increase in change within your societies, and even your media stories.

A huge push is now being made to begin solid change that will develop into the beginnings of that higher dimensional life which you so desire. Some incredible, from your viewpoint, technologies will become commonplace within your very near future. Those who will not be controlled by your power structures have found ways around those who would continue to block them.

We continue to hear many say that we should do more. And once again we say to you, not to accuse, but to instruct, that you need to be the ones who do more. Heaven, indeed, does have feet and hands, but they are in your shoes and gloves, dear ones.

And so we ask you to make a choice between involvement and patience. Lack of patience combined with non-involvement are not becoming to you. Now, we realize that not everyone can be physically occupied with, or even know about, all that is going on. It is a very big world when seen from your viewpoint. But when you daily offer your prayers, meditations, and intentions, you are involved.

Those who do that are not the complainers, you see. Offering your agreement with the goals and then doing nothing but asking for more help is hardly what we have asked of you.

We have said over and over that the changes that you wish to see will be reflections of changes within yourselves. Yet many make no such changes and then take heaven to task for not saving them. It is never too late to begin, my friends. But the time is soon to come when you may wish you had begun. You have lived long enough on your world to recognize that possibility for yourselves.

On a happier note, it is becoming more and more frequent that we see some of you having breakthrough experiences in consciousness and understanding. We have spoken in other forums of the possibility of this occurring for large numbers of you soon. This possibility is bearing down upon you rapidly. We know you feel the changes within more and more strongly. It is as if the final pieces of a puzzle are dropping into place.

This will be a year of good news, dear ones. Polish up your dancing shoes. Good day.

Today, as we have just discussed with this channel, we will begin an entirely new type of communication.

It is our intent, with his agreement, to begin an ongoing conversation concerning whatever topics are of the utmost concern to those of you who follow our message. It is true that each of you is unique and on a journey unlike any other in many ways. But it is also true that there are many very close similarities among you. There are many concerns, therefore, that you hold in common.

So we will, from today, begin a conversation with you that is ongoing and not divided into self-contained bite-sized pieces. You will, no doubt, have noticed that 'the message', if you think of it in that way, has been merging into a oneness of purpose across the globe no matter the channel we are using to express it. Differences in topic and wording do not keep the message from neatly dovetailing together into a wholeness. This is by design.

It is true, after all, that you are all on a path to the same destination. And although you all have to start from wherever you stand, many of the obstacles, and indeed victories, are the same for many, if not all of you. The planetary environment in which you find yourself is the same for all, even as the individual one is separate and unique. And the planned steps to be taken by the majority are often very much alike, as the energy envelope you are in and the current states of your consciousness are similar.

There is now developing, for instance, a growing awareness of the change in light quality, color, and energy around you. You are being urged, by us, to become aware of other facets of yourselves than you have ever given much thought to. Increasing numbers of you are having what seems like vast expansions of awareness and consciousness that are fleeting, but never to be forgotten. They leave you amazed and changed.

All of these things are there for you to explore. They are all stepping stones on your pathway. And please realize that your pathway, as we are discussing it, is internal. We are not going to be discussing what outer, meaning physical, steps you might take in your lives.

We fully understand that those are important to you. Your current life is the current focus of your being, and rightly so. But it is not the focus of our guidance, and will not be. Your outward steps will be determined by the being you construct from what you learn and become. And that is as it should be, as well.

We urge you now to give some consideration to the great and powerful steps you have taken in your recent past, as you see it. You need now to give yourselves credit for the people that you have become so that you will feel more of your ability to become those you *will be* after this amazing year you are entering.

There is a lot spoken of regarding the fields of light and energy through which you are passing. We have done a lot of that here, but we have spoken little of the fact that it would not be so had you not attracted it and its intensity with your amazing progress.

There is not one atom in your physical body that has not been affected by this. There is not one thought that has not been, in some way, modified. The possibilities and probabilities of your coming time have, and continue to be, changed. And you are learning that the guidance system best available to you, both collectively and individually, is your imagination and intent.

These are things that have always been true, but which most of you are only now becoming reacquainted with. So there will be quite a lot of things for us to expand upon. We will determine the course of our conversation by observing your course and progress. We will give you things to consider as we go. And we will let you determine what is most appropriate to you at those times.

But we urge you not to throw anything away out of hand. Perhaps build a "may-need-this-later" shelf in your mental attic.

We will not use our normal way of ending these messages today. Instead we will say, "Till next time."

Today our conversation will continue with a discussion of what your February is bringing.

There is a great deal of talk and speculation about this topic now. That is true because a great many people are able to feel the energy of great impending change. Even those without access to your news media, which doesn't tell you much anyway, or your internet are feeling the massive restlessness that is engulfing many of your societies. All are subject to the ever increasing floods of light that your planet is passing through. Everyone and everything has had, and is having, changes made to their energy make-up, and that is having more and more effect upon their physical and mental selves.

We can put all of that into one simple idea and have previously done so. But we will say it in several ways, because it will better get huge concepts across in your limited words. You are beginning to embody more of your true Selves. Your Higher Selves, that which we are, are now better able to express through you. You are raising your frequencies. The changes you have sought are manifesting. And we could go on and on.

This is being experienced by billions who have no idea of what we are speaking to you about. Be prepared for this. Think of the things which you know have happened to you, that you have felt, seen, or heard, and imagine what you would feel if you had no previous understanding. You might think you were going insane. You might refuse to even acknowledge it to yourself. Certainly, you would not talk about it. Many will react in unfortunate ways. But many more, knowing of your thoughts on such things, will come to you in a quiet moment and ask questions, trying to begin a conversation that they do not know how to have.

Now will be the time for you to use the deep understanding and love that you have learned to hold.

We can also tell you that the light and energy which has brought all of this forth, although it has been immense in volume and effect, is only going to keep increasing. We again bring out the metaphors we have used of waterfalls, floods, tides, and avalanches. This has begun now in earnest and your world **WILL *change*** because of it.

Now, it is possible that many may say, "We did those things." And we will say in return, "YES!" That is what we have been at pains to tell you for so long. It is not that someone on the earth did it as opposed to someone in spirit doing it, however. That separation does not exist. It is a concept, although an incomplete one, almost we had said erroneous. We act with you here, if here is a place, and act for us there. That is the way of it. And now you can do more here and we can do more there though you. And that will be the way of it.

We hope these thoughts make you cheerful and optimistic. This is certainly a time for which we have been working and waiting.

The point of this all is that we want you to start realizing the profound effect your combined thoughts, dreams, and actions have had and are having. We want you to feel your value to the

whole. We want you to begin to think of yourselves
AS the whole.

Now that is something that will take many
eons to complete, but you are making a start.

With love we say, "Till next time."

We have communicated with you now,
through this channel, for over two years. You have
been an audience that has both grown and
remained loyal as the clarity and purpose of these
messages have grown. Some have expressed
dismay that the messages have become fewer, even
though lengthier. At times this has been due to
much other work which has been begun, and this
will not be changed. We have, however, been quiet
here for almost this entire month. We have allowed
you to assimilate and to have a respite from the
energetic tidal wave, at least as much as possible.
Most of you have chosen to continue seeking
whatever information that you could find anyway,
and that is a good thing. It shows your
determination and dedication.

Now we return. This will be a rather short message, but not an unimportant one. The new sources you have found, or in some cases, come to rely more on, are telling you of the immense import and the impending change that is now upon you. We are here to tell you now that this is absolutely true. The universe is gifting you with an alignment of energy that has not been seen before. And the result of that will be what you have not imagined before. We are not giving you a warning. We are giving you an accolade. We are extending our sincere congratulations.

We do have one last thing to recommend to you at this beginning of your 'wild ride'. This is what you have asked for, prayed for, and worked for many, many lifetimes. You know by now that many of these things do not come to your physical selves without some discomfort. You know, also, that your nature is to feel discomfort and doubt when things begin to change around you. You know that there are those around you who are sure to sound all the alarm bells and raise all the fears that they are able. We, therefore, wish to remind you to visit your deepest inner selves and be in a place of acceptance, gratitude, and knowing that the result of all of this will be what you have intended and nothing else.

It will be the tiniest of beginnings, and yet, what occurs for each of you has the potential to be amazing. Open your arms. Open your hearts. And allow the full potential of what is yours to be accepted. Let gratitude be your watchword. It will not be so long now before we speak again. Good day, dear friends.

We are now moving into a very interesting time for those who have claimed as their identity that of lightworker. Now we say in some humor, that interesting times have been viewed as both a blessing and as a curse. Go ahead and chuckle. We intend a bit of lightheartedness. But even though we jest with you, this is as serious as a headache, as you say.

On some days, you feel that time is at a standstill, and you are making almost no progress at all. On other days you feel as if the world is spinning so fast it may throw you off. Is this not so? What you are feeling is waves of change. And you may be certain that change has occurred and is still happening in ever increasing intensity and amount.

Depending upon your reaction to this, you may feel elated or put upon. Please strive for the former. If you allow the feelings of discomfort, stress, and helplessness to overtake your feelings of gratitude and anticipation, you can imagine, without our help, what that will draw to you.

Now, the purpose of this message is to alert the sensitive ones among you that there is approaching, rapidly approaching, a period of greatly increased change, both physically evident and otherwise. And we are intending to have you move into an accepting and grateful state of mind, a mindset of great anticipation. Many, many of you have been feeling as if something huge has been just around the corner for some time. It is indeed. And the corner is just there.

Also, many of you are beginning to notice subtle changes in yourselves. Of course, you then tend to discount them or forget them. We remind you that your first reaction, if it is one of acceptance and gratitude, will bring more and greater change to you more quickly.

Now, in the present, many of you do practice this. We remind you, because the surf is about to come up, and the breakers you will experience will be easier to ride well if we prepare you first. Those of you who are well along to communicating with us yourselves have already gotten this message. We speak now to those who are unsure that they know what they know or who are just waking.

Know this above all else in these times; everything, and we do mean everything, is occurring in your highest and best interest, just as promised. You will be asked to go into fear, even terror. There is no bogeyman in the closet. There is only the new world you have created. Of course, there are those who are terrified of that, but do not let them control your mind. If you simply look at what you can see around you, you will see your world rapidly improve. As you see it change, congratulate yourselves for what you have accomplished.

So, polish your boards and get ready to ride the pipeline. Love and light to each of you.

Change is our topic for today. You are living in a time of great change. You have been hearing that for quite some time. You are living in the only moment in which change can be made. That is also something you should be familiar with. You cannot make any change in the future, nor can you make any in the past. The only moment you can change is this one, the present, and in so doing, you will alter all future possibilities. You may also alter the effects of the past.

We would point out, however, that the only change which we council you on is the change that you can make within yourselves. You may have some idea of the importance of that, but we assure you that your ability to foresee the vast reach that your personal changes will have upon the future and the extent of the effect upon the entire universe is beyond your understanding. Even upon your world and within your society, there is no way for you to see the effects your smallest action will have in its ripple effect upon persons you have not and may never meet. You discuss this at times, but have you truly 'taken it on board', as you say?

That should be enough to motivate you in your day to day activity and thought. But consider, also, that there is no way for you to understand what effect the slightest improvements you may make within yourselves will have upon the future selves you are becoming. You will become someone with whom you are not in least familiar, someone beyond your experience. A slight change in attitude, in your way of perceiving, of reacting, and above all, in your beliefs about yourselves, will radically change your future. In fact, it is the only thing that can do so.

So, as we have told you recently, our recommendation to you would be that you spare no effort in finding out who the true self is that you are beneath and behind all the little beliefs you have been taught to accept about yourselves. Who are you, really? What is it within you that is real, permanent, unchanging? How will you find that? What will you do when you know?

It is not something that you need to become. It is something that you are and that you have not yet seen nor felt. That is the true quest. That is your true purpose. And that, once found, will change your world.

It is clamoring to be heard now. It is closer than ever. Listen, feel, and know.

Change. Let's examine the change that you are in the middle of at this time.

Is it not somewhat inconceivable that a sea change in the planet's systems would be largely unmentioned in the media? Would you not expect that some discussion of anything of this magnitude would be happening? Is such a thing not more important than an annual basketball tourney or a reality television show?

The entire financial structure of your world is being radically modified. You are about to find that out whether or not you have been following these things. And the resultant effects upon your everyday lives will be enormous. That alone should be enough to excite everyone. But we tell you, once again, that the true miracle is that the changes in your consciousness, your frequencies if you will, are the true changes. Everything you see outside of you is illusion. All of it, no matter how real it seems, is destined to change, to cease to exist at some point. Why? Because you will change. You will grow. You will continue to create. Your true nature is to always strive for more and better. And you will always succeed. You always have.

Now that the truth of that is about to be undeniably demonstrated, you might wish to look inside at who you truly are and apply these realizations to your own lives. The real miracles, and the real miracle workers, are yourselves. Once you understand who creates the life you are living, you will have taken back your ability to make the changes in your own lives that you desire to make.

Sometimes it is more comfortable and convenient to be a victim of circumstance. But next to the thrill of achievement, it is dusty and tasteless. Find out who you are. Be your own hero. We are not speaking of the ego you, but of the feeling, knowing you that holds the spark of your Creator.

Look inside for the you that reacts when you are disrespected. Find the you that explodes in joy when you learn to do something new. Find the you that melts when you see a happy child or a loving animal. Find the one who lives deep in your heart. Allow that you to surface and live more and more through your actions feelings. Tell your thoughts that your ego is not in danger, but it does not need to be in control either. Give this new and growing self the chance to build a new life for you. As we have said several times in the past, amaze yourselves.

We have also told you that there will be efforts to scare you at this time. The sky is not falling. New wars will not solve anything. The end of the world is not at hand. Look at what is around you, not at your television set.

This short message is a bit off our usual message, but you have entered the time of rapidly cascading changes that we have spoken of so often before. The long period of delays has come to an end. That saddle that we spoke of before? Hang onto it! Congratulations.

Several times we have given messages regarding acceptance. Today we wish to discuss something that you may not have seen brought forward before—non-acceptance. This will give you an opportunity to employ the wisdom you have gleaned, even if you don't currently see yourself as having it. We see you, and we see that you, indeed, are far more than you believe.

At this time on your planet, there begins in earnest a time of clearing. It appears to you that everywhere you look there is the lower, the negative. What the actual condition is, is quite different from that. Consider this. There has been always great peace and beauty in your world. The predominant wishes of humanity are and have been for peace, love, and security. That makes the negative seem to stand out boldly from the loving background. Even more so is this true now, since so very many of you see the negative clearly and truly wish it were not a part of life for you and your loved ones. It stands out so clearly because, yes, it is so very negative, but also because there is so much contrast as the collective vibration is actually lifting. There is also the fact that there really is less of it. And add to that the fact that this is the time when it must and will be cleared.

Now, you may not be, probably are not, one who is actively engaged in activities that are removing such things from your reality. So what may you do? Here is where the non-acceptance, the practice of non-acceptance can come into play.

As you see or hear of things which appear less than desirable, along with the choice to perhaps cease listening or watching these things, say, "I do not accept this. I do not concur with this. I do not choose this for my world. I do not agree." In other words, make a choice. You have that power. You have that power. You have that power. Exercise your right to choose.

Now, we understand that you are more than likely not yet fully aware of the power that you do have and its effect. So we suggest that you begin learning to be in what may be, for you, a new mind-set or awareness. Begin training yourselves to be aware that while you may indeed be an individual, you are also a part of a large and powerful collective mind that has created the world in which you are living, and these choices do and will have an ongoing effect upon that world. Conscious choice is beginning to trump unawareness and unwillingness to see.

We have told you in many ways, and for a long while, that your inner change was the important part of the changes that are happening. But there has come a time, an inevitable time, when the effects of that begin to be seen and felt. Prepare to blow your own socks off. We do love your sayings. Good day.

Where are you now? Let us give you a bit of reassurance that some of the vague suspicions that have been hovering in the background of your minds are, indeed, correct.

Many of you have had repeated feelings that you were looking at things that were not exactly real; the wall, the floor, or those trees were somehow not as solid as you previously thought. Well, that is what the ancients and even your physicists have been telling you forever, is it not? So you might say that you are actually beginning to perceive reality for what it is.

Some of you are beginning to feel a presence, or presences, about you. We know there are those that have felt or even seen this for a long time, but we are speaking now to those who may even be wondering if they are 'losing it'. You are not losing it. We have spoken to you often of just these sorts of things, but they did not seem so immediate since they did not seem to apply to you personally. You are beginning to acquire the gifts that you have seen in others and thought you would never have. Well, you had them, but now your rise in frequency is causing them to surface.

If none of these things seem to apply to you, ask yourself if truthfully you have not begun to know things and do not know how you know. Have you noticed yourself reacting to something in a way that you never would have in the past? Have you already been experiencing things that you know are symptoms of your changing consciousness and physical make-up but now are noticing an intensification of them?

We wish you to know several things about this. You may feel alone because you do not discuss these things with others. In fact, you are now one of millions. There are people everywhere, speaking many languages, who are going through the same process. There are people who do not even know they are going through a process who are, nevertheless, experiencing the same things.

The world desperately needed change. You asked for change. Change has come. You also asked for, meditated on, and prayed for change that would not be cataclysmic. And so it is happening at a rate that will not destroy everything in its path, as has, indeed, happened before. And this change is a reflection of the change that is happening within yourselves, as we have been stressing to you over and over for quite some time. What you see when you look around is the sum of what you have all created. It is a mirror. If the image in the mirror begins to change, it can only be because all of you have begun to change.

Now you may have your change in ways that make you uncomfortable, if you wish. You never seem to want to go through change. You only want things to be changed. Or you can dance and sing in joy and gratitude. It is, indeed, up to you. We'll let you figure out which will be easier. It is not, as you say, rocket science.

Let us point out one more little thing before we stop for today. This ascension stuff is not being thrust upon you. It is being drawn to you by your own desire, decisions, and efforts. Many in this universe are in awe of what you are doing against all odds. That dancing and singing thing we mentioned may just be in order. May the unconditional love and blessings of the Creator forever be yours. Well, of course it already is. Good day.

Power

We said at the end of our last message that we would continue speaking of the source of your personal power. We shall do that. This is a topic that could be discussed at great length; so do not be surprised if we do not finish it today. We have decided to have you compare two different imaginary persons and let you discover for yourselves how the differences we propose would affect them.

For the purpose of this comparison, we give you a personality called John and another we shall name Ray. You will see that you know many who have similarities to John, and not so many, perhaps like Ray.

Now John thinks he is separate from everything else he sees around him or even imagines. John thinks he is religious, but his understanding of religion is that he could be condemned by his deity or saved from that by someone or some belief. John thinks that he has very limited power. His God is all powerful, but his God is separate from him. John knows that he is born a sinner and that he is also guilty of many other things that he is unsure he can be forgiven for. John knows he has only one life, and he must get it right. John's only hope is that his version of God is the correct one; therefore, he has to know that any other version cannot be. He clings to it like a life raft. John feels that he is mostly powerless to control his life. Life happens to him. We could continue in this vein for quite a long time.

Now let's look at Ray. Ray's understanding of reality is far different. Ray knows that everything he perceives, solid or otherwise, is really just differing energies. He can see that this leads to the understanding that nothing is really separate from anything else. That means to Ray that he is not at all separate from the energy of Creation. The energy of Creation is the source and substance of Ray's being. Ray knows that the only being in the universe that judges his own actions and thoughts is himself; therefore, he chooses to forgive himself and all others. Ray knows that every thought he has and every intent is what goes into producing the life he is leading. Ray knows that, since nothing is separate from him, his God and his Higher Self are a part of him and know his every desire, intent, and need. And again, we could go on and on.

Do you see how the two persons we are imagining would be living very different lives? Do you see how their beliefs would cause them to do so? Can you also see how the energy, the power, the love of Creation would flow unobstructed through one and not the other?

Now, so far we are discussing theories, correct? That is unless you personally identify with one or the other example. But we propose that you consider a decision to become more like Ray and far less like John. Move the discussion from theory to experience and see what changes happen in your life. We are not proposing that anyone change from one religion to another, but we are proposing a different understanding of the age-old principles involved in the beliefs that they are based upon. And the root belief of all? Try this on. The energy of my Creator flows through me. See how that might change everything.

As you might see, changing some of these root beliefs would cause one to act very differently in one's life. A lack of guilt feelings would give one more confidence. Knowing oneself as being loved unconditionally by Creation would give one an unshakeable self-worth. That self-confidence and self-worth would translate into very different responses to life. And think about the confidence of knowing that you are trusted enough to have been given, not only Creator's life energy, but the free will to use it however you see fit. At first that may seem like an awesome responsibility. But consider what it means as far as response ability.

These are weighty topics, are they not? And we promise we will be more lighthearted next time. But we felt that many who are awakening at this time are needing to get a big jump-start on their way. There is a lot of old baggage that may need to be tossed. This discussion today may serve to point out the why of that.

Remember, until next time, we are one thought away from you. Good day.

We said in our last message that we would be addressing the topic of soft power, of your power, of what and how you could best use the energy of the amazing beings that you are becoming. We shall do that. Now the channel should be aware that this is not a simple and short topic. There is nothing completely new that we shall be telling you here, but in this case, we wish to cover much more than we usually do in these short paragraphs. It has been the wonderful case that there are many reading these who are relatively new to the ranks of the awakening who need more information than those of you who are already well along in your understanding of light, energy, and how you personally use it. We trust, however, that you may read something you had not considered or that will be a welcome reminder.

First, let us explain that when we use the words light, energy, vibration, sound, etc., we are speaking of various manifestations of the same thing. For us, there is no inherent difference. In fact, for us, you appear as all these things yourselves. You have a unique light, a unique energy, a unique frequency, a unique sound that is you. We will be discussing the ways that you may use this to your best effectiveness for yourselves, for the collective, and for the entire self-aware universe.

Now, to begin, let us point out to you that, and your physicists will not argue with this, there is nothing, no thing, in the universe that is made out of anything other than energy. Your Einstein spent a lifetime proving that. Actually your Tesla was no second fiddle in the field either. So there is a universe in which you live, in which everything you observe consists entirely of energy, and energy is vibration, is frequency. Let's look at what that means. And it might surprise you, even though it is quite obvious.

It means that there is nothing that is not affected by every change you make in your own energy. All you need to make your own experiment for this is a couple of tuning forks, although there are a great many others you could do. You will be aware already that one tuning fork will set off vibrations in another, and that if they are compatible, ringing one will cause another to ring as well. Thinking of sound still, you know it expands in all directions from its source, but you need to realize that it is causing change in everything it touches. The same is true of all energy. It causes change in everything it touches. And this will be the basis for everything we discuss.

We will add another short note here. You are aware that in your dimension, distance from the source produces reduced strength of these changes. In other words, the loudness of sound diminishes with distance. And we will tell you now, that contrary to the obvious, the energy produced by change does not ever cease expanding outward, nor does it ever reach zero. You can change the state of energy, but you cannot un-create it. It just is. Now it may be an exaggeration to say that a butterfly moving its wings in Asia may cause a hurricane in Florida, but it does illustrate the point nicely. Every thought, every word, and every deed has an effect on everything, everywhere.

This is all very nice to think about, but what does it mean when we bring it back to you personally? Let's spend some time thinking about that.

Let us begin with a change you make in yourself, perhaps in how you react to something, perhaps in your beliefs system, in what you accept as true, or in your perception of your self-worth. Actually, these would all be interrelated. This would create a change in your personal frequency, in your energy itself. It would create changes in your DNA. It would create eventual physical change. All of this is easily understood by many people today.

Not so easily understood yet is that because of the unity, because time and space are really illusory, you will have actually changed all of your other aspects, your other selves, as well. Some of those are living what you perceive as past lives. Now, it is easy for you to understand that you can have an effect upon your future, but if you followed what we just said, you would see that the changes you make in yourselves also affect your past. That is contrary to the accepted 'knowledge', but it is true nevertheless.

Let us further bring in the idea that everything that exists, even all matter, is made of energy. All energy is conscious. Therefore, everything is aware and intelligent. You can easily understand that everything you perceive produces experience, and therefore, reinforces, contradicts, or teaches new concepts for you. It follows, therefore, that everything you or anyone else do, produces the same in everything that perceives it, and that is the All. That makes you a major change maker—a cutting edge learning tool for the Universe. Have you ever thought of yourself in that way?

Now, you could be somewhat daunted by such concepts, but we are almost certain that you are not. Almost everyone who begins to contemplate these thoughts also begins to understand that they are an invaluable and irreplaceable part of All-That-Is. It matters not what you do, how much you have, or any other of the measuring sticks that you have believed apply to you. You are a creature that is a facet and child of the Divine. Period. End of today's rather lengthy discussion.

The divine spirit that we are salutes the divine spirit in you this day. Namasté.

Let us now return to the subject of your use of the power that you have, the energy that you control. There are many ways that you can do this. There are many ways that you do this already. Some of what you do is intentional, and some is still unconscious. As you learn to accept that you can be intentional with these things, they will become, more and more, the conscious and intentional ways in which you interact with the world about you. We will tell you that your current ways of wishing, of asking, and of supplicating will evolve into intending and expecting as you learn to understand the power and effect that you have upon your surroundings.

Now, first let us be clear that every thought you have has some greater or lesser effect upon all of this. We will take it for granted that greater and intentional is something that you desire. Let's look at what does and does not increase your effectiveness in this regard. We will also assume that you are aware that worry and doubt need not be discussed, as they obviously will not have a beneficial outcome.

Wishing has an effect that moves one toward what one wants. It is not a very powerful effect, and it can be wiped out quite easily by wishes that counteract it or conflict with it, which you do all the time. Think of "I wish I could have such and such, but...". That little word 'but' cancelled out the entire effect of the thought. Doubting? Doubting that the desire could or might materialize has an instant counter effect.

So what does work? Simple steps, please? OK. Imagine, focus, communicate, expect. And do all of those clearly, simply, and consistently.

First, imagine what it is you want to see, have, or experience. Some use the word visualize. That confounds some people, as they don't think of themselves as seeing these things. So imagine it in whatever manner works for you. We know you know how to daydream.

Next, focus on it. Embellish upon it if you can. Since you are imagining it, you may as well imagine everything you can about it, including what it will be like to have it or experience it. What does it feel like, look like, sound like, smell like. How does it make you feel?

Now communicate your desire to the highest power you can imagine. But try not to fall into your old habit of asking or begging or pleading. Confidently expressing your intention would be very good. If you realize that you are actually speaking with something that is the biggest and best part of your own being, so much the better. If that is true for you, you can go ahead and command that it be done. Trust us when we tell you that BIG YOU will not mind at all when you do this.

And now comes the tricky bit. Expect it. One popular channel, coach, and healer says, "Expect miracles." That's not a bad idea. Another says, "Assume it will be." That is also good. Even singing the "Anticipation" song is good. But do NOT allow yourself to second guess it. If you like, return to it all you want and expand upon or enjoy the taste, feel, smell, and sight of it. It's yours. Know that.

And don't quit on it one hour before it happens for you.

What about bigger and better things? Well, creating a new world is really just the same as creating a house, or car, a new job, or anything else. After all, this energy you are speaking with created you, your world, and the entire cosmos. Is your imagining any bigger than that? So you can follow the same steps we just gave you; imagine, focus, communicate, and expect. But what about a short cut? Every time you learn something, you end up looking for an easier and better way, do you not? You want a short cut. Well, surprisingly, there is one. But there's a catch. There's always a catch, right? Here we go.

Now, first of all, let us tell you that this is something that you have all been remembering for a very long time. Notice we said remembering and not learning. None of this is new to any of you. That may not have been true before, but it is more and more true of everyone left on your planet now, and particularly those who read these messages. You know these things at some level, and we only remind you when you seek to know. We do not ask you to spend time and effort studiously putting these things into practice like a group of dedicated monks of long ago and far away. Read them. Allow yourselves to feel the truth of what we say if it indeed resonates with you. And then relax into it, and let it lead you.

There is, first of all, the concept that everything is energy, energy is conscious, and that is what you are made of. We have discussed this at length before. The joke here is that your scientists keep trying to figure out how matter produces consciousness when the process is exactly the opposite. Consciousness produces matter. But that is not our subject.

Now, we can describe energy in many ways. We can call some frequencies of it sound. Others we call light. Some are heat. Some are thought. Some radio. Some this and some that. But it's all frequency, and it's all what we call light. It is just a spectrum of frequency—if you can imagine that. So you are exactly that. You are a collection of different frequencies that express all of who you are, past, present, spirit, matter, emotions; the whole of what makes you you is made up of that. You are light.

Since that is what you are, why not become the highest and purest and brightest light you can imagine? Well, that is exactly what you all do to the best of your knowing and ability. You do. So let's help you increase that ability and bring back your knowing. Let's get you into such a high frequency that all of the stuff we discussed above becomes like what arithmetic is to a physics professor. At the highest frequency you can become, just being and intending the best is all you need. Said in another manner, bringing your loving consciousness to bear and allowing it to affect the world around you is all you need.

You are all ready to take this step now. It is within reach for all of you. The method? There are literally thousands. Pick the one that rings your bell, as you say. We will certainly give you one, but feel free to use another, if you choose. We said there is a catch, and there is. The catch is that you must trust the process. It is a process. You must trust it. You must start where you are. It is the path you are all searching for. The step you must take is your next step. You make things much too complicated. Keep on keeping on. Go with the flow. Do what you see to do. You are exactly where you need to be. That is true for each and all of you. If your aim is to rise, then rise you will. Nothing can stop you except yourself.

Now, back to those bigger and better things we were talking about. You will find, as you continue along the path we were just discussing, that the frequency that you have become has changed what needed to be changed as it was encountered. Short cut. Plain and simple. You are the change. You are the changer.

You are learning to remember who you are and not to believe that you are what you have been taught to be. You are the entire cast of this play and not the role you are in at the moment. You are the leading lady, the leading man when he got sick, the extra in act two that you had to be last night when they didn't show up, the director, and everyone else. And when you look at it from the perspective of the cast party, you can see and understand all of that.

We wish you to know that you are doing a great job. You should be very happy with yourselves, and you will be when you see what we see.

We said that we would give you a method, a simple method. We will continue with that next time, as this has become long enough, we think. Do give some thought to what we have said, and adopt it if you see fit. As we suggested, just relax into it. Play with the ideas. Good day.

We would discuss with you now the recent lifetime of one who has come home to us. Rather, we would discuss what he was able to bring to your attention, and offer a different perspective than what is generally perceived. We are referring to the master known to you as Masaru Emoto.

This one worked with water, and you usually think of him as showing you that water has consciousness and that it will take on and exhibit for you various forms showing the beauty or lack of same in your thoughts and words. And yes, he did do that. But there was far more importance in his message than that.

If you carry the theme of his work to its logical extreme, there emerges something far more wondrous. You are, most of you, at least somewhat familiar with the idea that you create your own world. You intellectually understand the concept. You may not agree with it all the time, but your mind can understand it.

What this work did was to simply and undeniably illustrate that your thoughts, words, and feelings do physically change the stuff around you. You can, and you do, indeed, create the world you live in. The stuff from which your surroundings are created are visibly influenced by those thoughts, words, and feelings.

Now, it is your turn. What are you going to do with that knowledge? You may let it lie and eventually, for the most part, forget it. Or you may decide that this is an idea that, when truly taken to heart, empowers you like no other. You no longer need to imagine that you have an influence on what is around you. You have seen it. He has shown you. He has shown you visible proof that what is in your heart and mind does, indeed, influence what is. You are that powerful. You are, in fact, so powerful that you do this without even trying.

Imagine how powerful you will be when you do it on purpose.

With unconditional love for who you are, we bid you good day.

Light and Energy

We continue today by speaking further on what, from your point of view, is incoming light.

Let us approach the subject from an entirely new perspective this time. We will speak in the language of linear time in order not to introduce additional confusion into the process.

It was known that new and vastly stronger energy, light, and information... those three being almost synonymous... would be needed to lift your world out of the lower energies in which it had been mired for so long. And it was needed that the changes be initiated and carried out as what you call an 'inside job' in order to do so without outside interference. So a call went out for volunteers to begin a long slow process of carrying in, receiving, and anchoring what was needed to get the job done. Metaphorically, you could think of that as what you call transceivers.

None of this is new, we know. Of course, since it would only appear so due to your not remembering, it is not new anyway. Now the process has resulted in more and more of you being here to facilitate this. And the changes you have made in yourselves have resulted in the ability of you, humankind, being able to handle, to embody, more and more of the light frequencies that were, that are, needed. And the design includes the increase of light as you are able to utilize it.

So here you are in the second month of a pivotal year receiving enough of the light, the energy, the information, the love of Creation to almost literally make your heads spin. Do you not just love it?

May we point out, also, that all of this is talked about in many other metaphorical terms in order to get across as much of an explanation as possible? And might we also point out that that sort of language is visual, almost dream-like? It is the language used in what you call your right brain. It is the language of your imagination. It is the language of telepathy. It is a language that has been downplayed, derided, and ignored for quite some time. And it is the language, we are at pains to point out, which the vastly major portion of your being uses and exists within. It is the key for which you have been searching, and yet you are trained to ignore it. Individually, you may want to reconsider that.

At this time, you are immersed in such powerful and vast amounts of this light that major change cannot be impeded much longer. It has, in fact, been in progress for a while, but you are not told much about it, as yet. Your best indicator is what is happening in and for yourselves anyway. That is what is most important for you, is it not? And that is easiest begun and carried out by yourselves.

We have been bringing that message to you for some time. The results of what you have done as individuals are now merging with those of others, and the effect is to increase the momentum overall. You are magnificent! And still you do not, as yet, see it.

So let us remedy that. Beginning now, every time you see the situations in your world improving or showing the potentials to improve, say to yourselves, "We did that." Because no matter what we say to you about light, energy, or unconditional love, the truth is, you did that. And you will do the rest of it, too. That is what is meant by co-creation. You change the All by changing yourselves. That is where your personal power comes from. It is the power of the All flowing through you.

We will have more to say on that topic next time.

We will speak today on a topic that we believe will bring new hope to many. Many of you have been immersed for several days now in what must appear to you like utter chaos. It will have seemed to you as if not only your worlds, but the entire world, has been turned on its ear. Let us discuss this phenomenon.

You will remember much discussion in the past regarding the influx of new energies and their effect upon you. We have talked of the raising of your own energy frequency and how it would bring up things from within to be cleared and released. All of those trusted channels with whom we communicate have spoken of this often. It is the case now that the tipping point has been reached and surpassed for many of you. A great load of baggage that you needed to be rid of has come to the surface, and you may now let it go for good. Do not go to 'baggage claim'. Just throw away your ticket, and leave it where it lays.

Now, assuming that you do that, what happens next? Well, that shiny new self that you have been trying so hard to construct will begin to surface now. Let that self come out to play. It may not feel exactly comfortable to you at first. No change ever does. You may actually be surprised at some things you might say or do. But some changes do not take long to become accustomed to because they are so very welcome. This is one of those. Be prepared to claim more of the good, loving, and happy things in yourself for yourself. Be prepared to like you.

This does not mean that all will be peaceful around you forevermore. We will tell you now that great and momentous alignments are still on your horizon. These reflect the conditions of your collective consciousness and will bring greater change yet. This will still be a tumultuous year. But it will be a period you will be very happy to have gone through when all is said and done. Many speak of all the things that they want to happen. Many speak of those things as if they can happen overnight. Even so, it should be obvious that were that to happen, you would be in for an impossibly wild ride. You should feel grateful that things will not be quite so dramatic as that.

We tell you again that nothing is happening without your input, even though you do not have the conscious memory of it. So you can be reassured that you are managing these changes in the best possible way. Despite all the clamor for instant change, things will be done in a bit more orderly a fashion. But they will be done, and the evidence of that is becoming more and more visible, both to those who await it eagerly and to those who dread it.

Now, speaking again of energies, let us mention before we end this that there is an energy afoot now that is growing, it is unstoppable, and it will wreak great and lasting change upon your planet, and indeed, this entire universe. It is an energy that has been awaited for twenty of your centuries. It has taken that long to mature in its effect, but it is here now. It is in you now. Do not seek it outside of yourselves. How often have we said that? But it is here. We are working with it. You are beginning to wield it. Some have called it soft power. That is as good a name for it as can be, although it has many others. Unconditional love is another.

When we continue, we shall speak at length about what that means and how you might best utilize it. For now, take a brief respite after such a demanding few days. You have done well, and we love you and support you in all things. Good day.

We have spoken in our last message of ways, methods, to increase your frequencies. We will bring some of them forward today. Let us state beforehand that we are not going to give you anything that is new. After all, you have been on this path for thousands of years, and many ways of doing this have been developed. You were the ones who developed them. So we will jog your memories. We might give you a thought or two about them that may be other ways of thinking that you have not considered, but the practices are very, very old. They are well used. In the manner of wearing a pathway through a forest, that is a part of their efficacy. There is no need to re-invent the wheel. There is no need to blaze a new trail.

We will speak of light, which is high frequency energy. We will speak of grounding. We will speak of your perceptions and understanding. We will recommend that you begin a daily practice if you do not currently have one. We also recommend that you do not beat yourself up for not having one or for missing a day in your daily practice if you do have one. Remember the whole purpose is to raise your frequency, and beating yourselves up will certainly not help that. Let us begin.

We mentioned light as a frequency of energy. We would now remind you that we have recently spoken of all energy as being a total spectrum and what you perceive as light as being a portion of that spectrum, as is sound, heat, etc. But for the purposes of this discussion, let's simplify things by referring to light, energy, love, and the 'ground of all being' as being synonymous. We will make the terms interchangeable.

It is being said by many sources, and correctly, that you are in a process of increasing your physical body's capacity to hold higher and higher frequencies and amounts of that light which we have just defined. If you are upon this planet at this time, you already have managed to do quite a bit of this. Some do it quite well and painlessly. For some, it is problematic. We have been at pains to mention frequently the uses of acceptance, gratitude, intention, grounding, etc. as ways to minimize the effects of this upon your mental and physical selves. Some who are having problems do not even suspect any of what we are discussing. Others, in their rush to accomplish their purposes, have 'bitten off more than they can chew', as you like to put it. It is possible to catch up, and it is possible to dial the intensity back. These are things we can help you with.

We also mentioned grounding. The benefits of this can hardly be overstated. There are many ways this is being promoted now, from the simplicity of walking barefoot on your earth, to the relatively expensive 'earthing' movement and its products. All of these things are quite beneficial. What we wish to mention now is that you will need to center yourselves in your hearts and then visualize a connection between you and your planet as often as you can.

Returning to the topic of the universal energy itself, we wish to explain, in one place, some concepts that have been mentioned before lately in order to solidify understanding and expand it a bit.

The light, energy, healing, unconditional love, etc. which a great many of you invoke daily, is a oneness. It is, in its fullness, the I Am. It is conscious. It is intelligent. And you, in your varying ways of invoking it, are raising the frequency signature of everything around you as you raise your own frequencies. Allow us to repeat that, *as you raise your own frequencies*.

You may, of course, direct the light you invoke to anything or anyone you choose, but your simple invocation alone will change you and everything else as well. You may invoke it, bask in it, and be at peace, and know that you have left nothing undone. It will, however, as is well known, follow your intention. You may send concentrations of it to parts of your own physical beings, to emotions, situations, other places, other people, other things, or even situations. What you cannot do is specify outcomes that are in opposition to the free will of others or that would violate their chosen paths and contracts. It would be far better for your own progress to let the light itself figure out what is needed, and that is the point we intended to make with this entire paragraph.

Also, please understand that when you set aside time to do these things, you are not so much bringing your guides, teachers, and whatever term you personally have for the Deity closer, as you are bringing your awareness into alignment to what is already around you and a part of you. Again, let us repeat ourselves. It is a part of you. It is never somewhere else. It never goes away. We never do not hear you. We never do not know how you feel. And you are NOT judged, except, as we have told you before, by yourselves.

If you began reading this, you were very likely one of those who are on your journey of ascension. Since you have read this far, we are sure you are. So let us now express our deep thanks for your service to the All and assure you that you are held in love and great appreciation. We shall continue our dialogue another day.

Those of you who are able to sense these bursts of energy should be aware that this year, the increase in intensity will be greater than ever. Coupled with the fact that your base energy signature on the planet is higher than ever, this will make for an interesting time. It is time for you to give some thought to this part of the mechanism of change. These energies arrive in your neighborhood and change the frequency of everything, literally everything, on your world.

This includes each and every cell of your being. You are then experiencing a rise in the mental and emotional fields of your being, as well. Your consciousness is increased in quality, content, and effectiveness. This accelerates the changes in your outer world.

Now obviously, it is much more apparent to those who are aware of what is happening. Those who are totally unaware are experiencing greater and greater stress. Many, however, are reaching the threshold of awakening and beginning the journey which most of those reading this have already started. If you are one of those who count yourselves as awakened, then you should also be aware that your journey has just begun. There are universes, yet unknown, for you to explore, not the least of which is the one inside of you.

We ask you now to refocus on who you truly are and how your being here serves the whole at this crucial time. Understand that it does do so. Even the simple fact that your energy is rising is serving to help raise the vibration of the entire planet. But it is also true that you bring many other needed things to the table. You may be a leader of society. You may be the mother of children. Each of you is contributing something vital. It is not possible for you to see the far, far reaching effects of everything that you do and say. But you are changing a world and the history of this universe. That is an immense and worthy thing.

We ask you now to continue to find those things, those practices and ideas that will raise your consciousness further each day. Seek also, those understandings that will improve your health, for you cannot be as effective if you are not well. Know that fears, feelings of unworthiness, resentments and anger, especially if they are repressed and unexamined, are detrimental both to your health and your progress. Find ways to discover them and release them from your lives.

There is much great change in the making on your world. You will need all of the centering and calming skills which you have learned. But keep always in mind that the outcome will be far more wonderful than your imaginations have been able to see. As you love to say, just keep on keeping on.

We love you and are always, always in your hearts and in your service. Good day.

We have said that as the position of your planet relative to your star approaches, what will produce for you the phenomenon you call equinox, we will address the rising frequencies and intensity of energy that you are experiencing. And we will do so, although this is a topic that is frequently spoken and written of. We will approach it from a slightly different perspective, one of our favorite words, to give you a larger picture.

Consider, firstly, that you are rising above the plane of the galactic equator for the first time in a very long time. This is putting you in a very different energy than you have been in for about twenty-six thousands of your spirals about your star. As you move further and further above this equator, your frequencies will change more and more.

Secondly, you have plunged into a belt of photonic light which is increasing moment by moment as you pass deeper into it.

And then there is the subjective to think about; your own change. Each of you is in the experience of change that is being facilitated by these cosmic changes. Are the cosmic changes causing your changes, or are your changes reflected in your environment? It is an organic thing, you see, a chicken and egg sort of thing. The question only can be asked if one assumes that you and the cosmos are two separate things, and that is not the case.

The voice that speaks to you, and the you that hears the voice, are not separate.

Now, back to energy. It is experienced by most of you as intensifying. And it is the case that as each of you progress, and as your Self reaches out for more light, it is now available. Some of you feel it physically, some do not. Some hear it, some do not. Some see changes in the light, some do not. And that is because each of you is unique. Each if you are building a structure, a life, which is in a unique state and serves a unique purpose. You each serve the ALL in your own special ways. Some are solidifying the basement. Some are laying stones several courses up from the ground, and a few are re-finishing the attic.

Please refrain from comparing one to the other. That is dualistic judgment. Just understand that all are working together for the benefit of all. You are not more than, nor less than, the other. And neither is anyone else. Simply take joy in, and give thanks for, the progress you are making. Help each other when asked. Love each other always.

And so we end our almost mandatory discourse on energy for this equinox. We end with this reminder that we are always with you, and our purpose is always to both guide you on your path and aid you in all possible ways when we are asked. You are deeply and unconditionally loved. Good day.

There is information coming to you now through many channels and many of your sensitive writers, blog posters, and those on your social networks regarding a further increase in the energy, in intensity and frequency, as you move into this last month of your current year. This is true, and we would comment upon it through this writing, as well.

A part of the feeling of intensification that you are having is the relatively new aspect of activation of your internal abilities, many which you have been, up to this point, unaware of. You may have wanted to try this or that thing in the past but felt that you would be unable to be 'any good' at it. We are not going to tell you that you may be artistic masters in hiding, although you may be. What we are wishing to suggest is that the effort to find out will unlock the energies of creation that may be left dormant and blocked by disuse.

You are creators. Some of you can paint. Some can play music. Some can cook. Some can invent. And we could list many, many other ways that you can bring new things into being. You will find satisfaction in these things which you may not have ever felt if you have not exercised these creative 'muscles' before. You will also activate a little thing called inspiration. We will tell you simply and directly that this is yet another way for you to tune in to the part of you that is on our side of what you call 'the veil'. In many cases, the result may be something not seen before as you embellish upon the concepts and ideas that you find yourselves able to access. This you commonly call invention. World changing things have always come about in this way. And the environment or climate of that energy is enhanced as more and more participate in it.

So, that new recipe you're thinking of will contribute. Do not continue to undervalue what you do. Do not continue to undervalue what others do. Celebrate yourselves and congratulate each other. Lift each other in every way that you can, every day that you can. That new world you want?... this is how you are building it.

Back to that energy that we see so many more of you feeling. Tap into it. Intention and attention will do that. Some of you will try to direct it. Some of you will allow it to flow. Some of you will produce Mona Lisas. Some will produce great pastries. Some will find new healing methods or new meditations. Some will think the results are not so great. These are value judgments. The value is really in the creating. Change something and create again. That is how new worlds are made.

As humans strike out into new territory now, we urge you to do the same. And we urge you to feel yourself as a part of this. Learn to think of yourself and feel yourself as a part of the whole and not the separate being that you have been taught to value so highly. Feeling separate has its costs, as many of you have become aware. Feeling yourself as a part of the All, that is something to aspire to. Do what you do as a contribution. It will be a contribution, but your intent is what will be important for you. Good day.

We return today to one of our favorite topics: energy. We hope to give you a slightly different view of what is happening during this vital time. For some of you, this will ring truer than true. May the good Dr. Seuss pardon us. For others, it will still remain, for the time being, as something of a desirable possibility. And of course, there are those still who are in denial or are completely unaware as yet of the subject at all.

We are aware that some of you are able to see the energies that we speak of. Others of you have become very able to feel physically the waves of this as it pours into your bodies and environment. And there are myriad permutations of these abilities. Some are also sensitive to the changes that they observe in their bodies and their surroundings. Some others are once again feeling themselves on some undefined precipice. Something big is happening, but you don't know what it is.

You have, in the recent past, experienced other such moments, each one energetic in nature, each one easily able to go unobserved by those around you. Yet, to you, as you look back over these last years, each marking stepping stones of change and growth. You will think that you cannot 'put your finger on it', as you say. But you know that somehow, you are not at all the person you were just short years ago.

Each of these markers has been of increasing intensity and effect. And if you had experienced the last one at the first, you would have had trouble assimilating it into your lives, even if you were at all able to do that. This has all been planned out very well. And you know by now that we will tell you that you were a part of the planning committee.

Now, at the end of this year, you are fast approaching another of those markers. You have noted another unique alignment in your heavens and are calling it a portal, a doorway. Understand that what you observe on the outside is a reflection of what is on the inside. We say this over and over. Your heavens reflect you as much as you reflect them. All is inseparable. All is one.

What is happening is that you have all, recognized or not, reached a milestone in your evolution of consciousness, this one more intense than those before, just as they were. And now, the effects of your changes are becoming less and less deniable. Certainly, they will become obvious to you, even if not to all.

There are many groups coming together for meditations at this time, and that is a good thing, of course. We would like to move into a slightly more light-hearted energy now, and as we have done before, offer you an enjoyable image to hold as you think about what you are doing.

You have what you call thrill rides. On some of those rides your carriage gets pulled for a short distance as it reaches the summit in preparation for the plunge that brings your stomachs up into your throats. There is that slow click, click, click, and you know what is coming. The slightest of pauses... and then...

Well, get ready because that is where you are now, even though you may only see it in hindsight.

This has been, from your perspective, a long, slow process. We offer our deepest and most sincere congratulations on your perseverance and dedication. Celebrate yourselves. Good day.

It Rings True

Self Love and Worthiness

We are here today to bring your attention to the topic of self-love. We return to this over and over because it so important. Perhaps today we can give a different perspective of the subject and make it a bit easier for you to understand and move into the energy of it more readily.

When you think of the word love, your current understandings are weighted down quite heavily with ideas of romance, sacrifice, impossibly long lasting emotions, and all the other baggage that has sold so many songs, films, books, and television programs for many, many years. The love we speak of is not an emotion. Some languages have no word for the idea of love that your society has promoted for so long. That seems so strange to you. In your past, there were, in other languages, many different words to define many kinds of love. That also seems strange to you. But we speak of the energy that is the very stuff of which everything that is, is composed of. Now we know, that in your current intellectual understandings of the make-up of the universe, that makes no sense at all. You have been taught to think of the cosmos as a giant mechanism that can be explained and measured. It cannot be, but that is not important here.

Back to self-love. It sounds to you as if we are speaking of something selfish. We are not speaking of a self-centered spoiling of oneself. In fact, it is quite the opposite. And that is because you will achieve this only by understanding who you are, and that will completely change how you think and how you act. All that is needed for this to happen is for you to accept, finally, that you are a divine creation of the Divine and for you to stop judging yourself, to forgive yourself for all of those thoughts, words and deeds that you are so afraid of. No, they are perhaps not so very wonderful. But please understand that by experiencing them, you have actually learned that.

Now let's take a short moment to examine the judgment itself. If one says, "I am undeserving of my God's love because I have done this", then one is saying that a portion of the Divine, the All-That-Is, is undeserving of love. Is that not true? And so you are pronouncing judgment upon something that even the Creator does not judge. Now where is the value in that?

In contrast to this, how do you feel you would act if you knew absolutely that you were a perfect creation of God and were loved unconditionally, were forgiven for everything you had ever done, and were trusted to and beyond the limits of your understanding? What that would be is a complete acceptance of the love that is, and always has been, yours.

Here is a puzzle for you. There is no easy or quick answer for this. But it is a puzzle worth thinking about for a bit. Why, do you suppose, has this been so difficult for humans to accept? Have they been taught not to do so? And if so, why is that? Are they afraid to do so? And if so, why is that?

Is there really a spark of the Divine within you? Do you believe that? Can you own it? What will you do with it? Can you love it? Do you believe it loves you?

These are weighty questions, are they not? We ask them because we are very desirous of your knowing yourselves finally as we know you to be.

Let us finish with one final thought. It is time. It is time. It is time. Good day.

Having just spoken of self-love, let us move to the topic of worthiness, of self-forgiveness, of knowing oneself to be deserving of all that one can imagine. And we say all that one can imagine, because by and large, you do not imagine very big. You have, most of you, an ingrained practice of thinking you do not deserve very much. And you also have the habit of thinking that the big things are impossible for you.

Let's take care of that little misconception right now. There is available a force that has created everything that you can see and far, far more. For such a force, creating all that you can imagine is no more difficult than creating one flower, and both are miracles, are they not? So just for fun, why not practice thinking big?

Now please ask yourself, "Why do I think I don't deserve everything I need?" There are as many answers to that as there are people, but the most common is that you have been conditioned for a very long time to think that way. And you have been told outright that you do not deserve it. And you have believed it. You have imagined all the ways you might not deserve it, and you have believed that, too. You also believe that you carry sacks and sacks of guilt around with you. And we could go on in this vein for a very long time. So let's do a little thought experiment. You know, the kind of thing your Mr. Einstein used to do. It will be short, so let us propose it, and then you close your eyes and do it. And if it doesn't feel real, then do it over every day until it does.

Here we go. You are standing in front of your Creator. Now first off, He/She is unconditionally loving. Know that. There will be no smiting and damning going on. There will be a lot of loving, however. This next part is for you to feel, Creator's part has already been done, but you need to know that. So "Creator (or whatever you call Her/Him), I am sorry for all the things that I have not done perfectly, both remembered and not remembered. Will you please forgive me?" You know what the answer is, do you not? "Creator, I forgive everyone and everything that has ever done anything that I have not liked. I still may not like it, but I know that it has gotten me where I am today." And lastly, "Creator, I forgive myself for not being everything that I have been taught I must be and have fallen short of. I forgive myself for judging myself, your creation, as less than perfect. I forgive me. I forgive me. I forgive me." Now, come back to yourself and promise to find something to feel good about today. Find something to like about you. It shouldn't be too hard. After all, Creator loves you.

So do we, you know, always, always, always. Please begin to think of yourself as one who deserves everything that the universe provides, no less. We tell you that no one less would be where you are at this time. Good day.

It Rings True

.

Your Divine Nature

As promised, we will speak of why these messages, meaning those we send through this channel, as well as others, resonate with you and where they are meant to take you.

Now, if we were to ask each of you why these messages resonate with you, as you say, we would very likely get a variation of 'because I recognize truth in them'. That is more or less the meaning of 'resonates with me', is it not? And you might stop inquiring at that point. We ask you to look much deeper, and we do that in order to lead you deeper into your understanding of who you are. This is critical to your progress. At some point, you must finally learn and celebrate who and what you are.

Allow us to offer just one further idea for you to consider, if we may. The truth that you recognize is not a truth that you were taught as a child. It is not something that was universally accepted in your family or peer group. What is happening is that when you see such truth, such a concept, your inner Self, Higher Self, True Self, and thus this Council itself, is saying YES! Now it may take many forms, depending on what will best get through to you at the time, up to and including chills and 'truth bumps'. But you are being led, all of you, to a far greater understanding of what it is to be you, and that for the very best of reasons. You are in the midst of a very important time, and you have a very important job.

Now, before that little tidbit sends you off on flights of grandeur or into depths of despair, let us give you a bit of comfort. While some of you may, indeed, have involved yourselves in tasks of seeming great import, **THE** task of great import of which you are all a part is simply to be, at long last, the fullness of what you were created to be.

Let all the hoopla of how that is or is not happening and why fall away. Just make it your priority, your intense focus, to complete that journey. If you can do that, all the rest will fall into place.

We used a short phrase above that we would revisit in order to bring it into your consciousness in greater focus. We said, "your inner Self, Higher Self, True Self, and thus this Council itself". Did you catch that? We know we have said, here and other places, many times over the past years that we are always with you. It is the truth, you see, that we are, in fact, as much a part of the One as you are, and you are as much a part of the One as we are. We are not, and cannot be, separated from you. There are no secrets. There are no prayers unheard. There are no prayers unanswered. There are more than a few answers unheard, but that is another subject.

In today's context, if we may point this out, this means that we are sending you a message, through the voice or writings of another, and then we are hollering "Yes" in your ear, or heart, or gut when you receive it. That is what you call 'resonate'. Make the connection, and you will see that you are far more sensitive that you are giving yourselves credit for. Make the connection, and you will begin to understand that you are receiving from us yourself.

And so, where will this all lead you? It is intended to lead you to more and better communication between yourself and your Self. It is ultimately intended to bring you to a far greater realization of just who you are, of who and what humanity is. This is our purpose and our entire focus at this time.

Now, in order to help you along and motivate you further, let us agree with your understanding that you will pick up some rather interesting capabilities along the way. We offer, however, that it will serve you best to treat these as useful tools and not as goals in themselves. Keep as your goal the expansion of your consciousness and raising of your frequencies. The rest will take care of itself.

This is enough for one day, we think. Your equinox approaches. There is a rise in frequency and intensity. Perhaps we will visit his topic when we return. Good day.

More than a few of you have commented upon the seeming difference in the tone, the vibration, of the channelings that are coming through to you now, as opposed to those of just weeks ago. We would spend this one message in commenting upon that, if you will allow us. It will be a rather short post, as the explanation is quite simple. But we want to make it clear enough for you to accept it in its entirety, since that acceptance alone will raise you to quite another level of self-understanding.

You have been, and are being, lead to a greater understanding of what the truth of your being is. You are being lead to discard the old and false understandings of yourselves as small, as insignificant, as victims, as powerless. You've received gentle and often repeated messages that have stressed your divine nature. You have been told over and over again to look for your answers inside.

Now, there are still a great many of you who still have only a vague, even doubting, concept of this. However, this is changing, as more and more of you are coming to understand a bit of what this means and are seeing the changes that it makes in yourselves and in your lives. As one of you raises your personal energy signature, if we may term it that, it has the corresponding effect of raising the overall energies, as well.

What we are telling you is that the new level of teaching that you are receiving is in very large part due to the level of understanding that you have reached. Just as you could not learn mathematics in what you call pre-school, we adjust these messages to your progress. There is also the factor of the increasing clarity and abilities of those whom we have been able to use as our contacts.

This leads us to mention your own increasing discernment, another often mentioned subject. Your ability to feel the difference between truth and falsity and the degrees thereof is also a large factor. You choose which messages to read or listen to. This is your right, and indeed, your responsibility. And we will say, at this point, that many of you are doing an increasingly excellent job of making those choices.

So, what we are telling you is that your own awakening is making it possible for us to speak more plainly and explain in more direct ways the things that are necessary for you to know, when you need to know them. This is being done for you, as you need it, as you have agreed. We wish you to give as much credit to yourselves as you deserve. You are each a part of this awakening. You are a driving force, if you will. And we would have you remember that and begin to feel in yourselves the contribution that you are making. You are each of you an irreplaceable piece of this grand puzzle.

We hold you each in unconditional love and Creator's light. We are closer to you than your own thoughts. We are one.

We seem to have struck a chord! We see that the quote from our former message that is titled 'Your Divine Nature' has resonated well with many readers. We have decided, therefore, to expand a little upon that subject. It is time to do this now, as many more of you are becoming open to possibilities of the truth of your being that you would not have been receptive to not so long ago.

Now, lest we awaken your egos to their feelings of importance, let us remind you that everything you see around you is created of divine stuff. So don't get too puffed up. Your house pet is a divine being, too.

The problem is that you have allowed yourselves to believe the fiction that *you* are not. And then you even embellish upon that. You are too this, too that, and not enough of the other. And your belief in those things actually produces what you picture. You might say that your DNA and your cells say, "OK. We can make that for you." Quite a remarkable endorsement for your co-creativeness, wouldn't you say? But perhaps a teensy bit off in its usage.

But what we wish to discuss in relation to your divinity is that it is always, always with you. It is who you are. And what you feel is the measure of your alignment to it. Feel good about something? Aligned. Feel bad? Guess what!

Now to the point. Everyone, every person that you meet in your daily lives, is a divine being, as well. You may not like what they say. You may detest what they do. But the fact remains that they are a divine son or daughter of the Creator that is learning tough lessons, just as you are. It is entirely possible to love the divinity in them and still not approve of their words or deeds. And it is not incumbent upon you to spend time in their presence. It is yours to love them and to forgive them.

Do not forget, also, that it is yours to love and forgive yourselves for what you think, say, and do. But learn from it. You will anyway, but it will be faster if you do it now than if you wait for what you call the afterlife to do it. Afterlife? How can anything be after something eternal? You see how even your language refutes what you say that you believe?

And so, if you find yourself having trouble feeling good about someone, look past what they are saying and doing and do your very best to see their true self. See their pain, their struggle. See that they are trying to cope with something you cannot see. Judge the act, if you must. But do not judge the soul. Send that soul love and light. In that way, you and the other will benefit from your experience.

We see a great many of you already do this. So please excuse us when we address things for the benefit of those around you that are being newly awakened. They are eternal beings, too. But now their time has come. And this will be true for more and more dear souls, and that, very, very soon. Look around you and see if you do not see huge change developing. Look inside and see it even more clearly.

As it has been said over and over again, it is you and the time is now.

We would speak with you on this day regarding several concepts that underlay our messages during this time. These will be familiar to many of you. They do, however, bear repeating. And it is also good for those who are aware of these things to remember that each and every day more of those around you are awakening and will need to begin remembering, will need reminding.

And why do we say reminding? That is because these are things that are very much an integral part of the masterful beings that you are, but which most of you were unable to take with you in your awareness when you were birthed into form. As you rise in frequency, you will become aware of these things, but we wish to aid you in doing so and thereby help the entire planetary consciousness in its journey. This is incrementally increasing in upward velocity day by day at this crucial time.

Some of these concepts are these: You are divine beings, masters who have agreed, indeed requested, that you be allowed the opportunity to be present at the time of this awakening. And as masters are exactly what was needed, you were granted this request. There were billions of slots to fill, many of which were not going to be comfortable in the slightest, and yet you did not shrink from the tasks. Your efforts are honored and appreciated, and the time will come when you know that. Also, know that there is nothing needed where you are that is not available to you. Each of you has had many, many lifetimes from which wisdom and experience, knowledge and ability, can be drawn.

We wish you all to know, also, that this Council, who is speaking to you now, is always available to you when and if you request our help. That is, and always has been, our function and reason for being. Whatever your need is or may be, it is possible for us to fill. If the specific holder of the knowledge or experience necessary is not with us at the time of your request, they will be, and instantly. There is nothing, and we repeat, nothing, that may be needed for this monumental task that will be withheld from you.

Also, please know that you are now accompanied, are in the company of, millions of others all across your planet who are receiving these same messages in whatever language they understand and in whatever images are compatible with their cultures. You are most definitely not alone.

We spoke repeatedly over the last several years of a snowball effect. We used images of floods, tides, and avalanches. We know that many of you now are feeling the accuracy of these descriptions as the Great Change picks up pace now. Remain steadfast in your intent and focus a bit longer. You will not be disappointed. All that has been promised by you, to you, will be yours. We say 'by you' because you are a part of this Council.

We will continue to impress upon you these reminders of what you have done and are doing. We do this so that you will begin to remember who you are, so that you will take heart and appreciate yourselves all the more. While your humility becomes you, your thinking less of yourselves does not. You are co-creators with the Source, the All-that-is, the I AM. Many of you understand this concept somewhat. Our goal is that you remember it in the very depths of your being. And what you are, the one next to you is, as well.

Many on this Council have spent lifetimes where you are in order to bring these concepts to you. Many of you have done this also. It is gratifying to see these ideas and ways of being begin to blossom so widely. We thank you. It is a joyous thing. Good day.

Let us have another conversation now about your finding the truth of who you are. You do tend to play your roles somewhat small, you know. And this hardly serves you nor the world you live in very well. We are not trying to inflate your egos. We simply want you to give yourselves credit for being capable of much more than you are doing.

Now, you quite often are told that you are this or you are that. You are told that you are the Christ consciousness or the Buddha mind at work in the world. True though that is, it does not seem to register with too many, and that is a sad thing. You have been taught carefully that you are 'only' this or 'just' that, and you have absolutely bought into it. 'Johnny never achieves his potential' is written all over life's report card.

There are many ways to begin uncovering that potential, but no one can achieve what does not seem possible for him or her. You must be able to see yourselves as you truly are. How can you do that? Again, there are many ways. But let us show you one that is very, very simple and easy to do. It is not as if the knowledge is hidden deep, deep in some well of unconsciousness and difficult to access. It is truly just below the surface of your knowing. It is hiding in plain sight, as you say.

Look in the mirror—not the glass thing hanging on your wall—the one that surrounds you every moment. Your entire surroundings are an out-picturing of your inner being. You have very likely heard that before, too. But what use is it?

Let us give you a way to use it very easily. You want to find out the wonderful, powerful, loving and caring person that you can be? Look at those around you with new eyes. Look at those you admire and love and value. See them. Really see them. Now, let us tell you why exactly they make you feel so good. They bring out in you qualities that you possess so that you can recognize them.

Work with that. We will help. Just make a beginning. This is the time when you are learning to embody SELF. Allow her, allow him, to surface and be accounted for here, where she/he is needed. It is your purpose for being here at this time.

Every day you ask us, "Why am I here? What should I be doing?" There is no mistake. There is no accident involved. You are where you need to be. You have everything you need. Just be all that you can be. Do what is before you. That will make possible more. Another step will appear. Another door will open. It may not seem miraculous. But then again, it may. You did not return to earth in order to live someone else's life. Live yours. And live it joyfully and well. You are the one who is needed where you are. Good day.

What will you create today? You are a creator being, fashioned in the likeness of the Being who created you and given free will. Let's explore, for a short while, some of what that might mean.

Let us begin by stating that you will create something. The one thing that you cannot create is nothing. You will have thoughts. You will make decisions. You will have experiences, and you will form opinions. You may decide to actually turn some of your thoughts into physical things. But even though that is likely how you think of creating, all the rest is creating, as well.

Now you can use some of your energy to look upon those things as good or bad. You have, of course, the ability and the freedom to do that, to judge what you have done. And when you do that, you are also quite likely to judge yourself for having done those things and even for judging yourself. And then you have also created what you call a vicious circle. Good name. They are vicious.

You also have the freedom to choose to use your best efforts to make every thought and every word, every action, to somehow improve something for someone or everyone. Will you make mistakes? Yes, you probably will. You are always learning. You are always able to look back and see things you might have done other ways. And you can fall again into the judgment thing. Or you can just decide to do it the other way next time. You can use the ability to see better ways to make new choices instead of spending time and energy beating yourself up for what is already done, thereby turning the experience into the cause for something of higher energy.

What is good, you can increase. What is beautiful, you can increase. What is of benefit to yourself, to others, to the All, you can increase. This is a decision that you may make and pour your life into. And when you do that, you raise the energy of absolutely everyone and everything. There is nothing that will not benefit from that decision.

So what are we saying here, really? We are saying in a rather roundabout way so that you can get a slightly better grasp on it, that you are a divine being of immense power. The extent of the effect you have on your world, not one atom of which you are separate from, cannot be known by you... yet. At the present time, your conscious awareness is not great enough to hold all of that. But, if you have come to trust what we tell you, then, as you say, you can take that to the bank.

And the time is soon to come that will have your awareness and abilities so far beyond what you have known that you will be hard pressed to believe it. In fact, believing it is what you are learning to do. If you can believe it, you can learn to be that new you that you have been talking about for a while now.

And we have now come back to the original question. What will you create today? What will you contribute to the field of consciousness in which you have your being? How will you respond to what is before you? The choice is yours, but you will need to begin where you stand. You may wish to begin somewhere else, but that isn't going to get anywhere. You have the honor, the privilege, and the ability to build from where you are. Go for it!

Consciousness

We will illustrate today's message by asking you to picture a drop of water falling into the bottom of a wooden bucket. Now this drop does not realize that she is not alone, but in fact, will be followed by two more drops, as will each of them. As the first drop lands in the empty bucket, it splatters. And it seems as if the effect is only a small damp spot on the bottom of the bucket. And then the two following drops land in widely spaced spots. There is still no apparent buildup of water in the bucket, but now there are four more drops on the way.

This is very much a good illustration of the awakening you are a part of at this time. Of course, there are many more than two whom you will affect. Let us carry this illustration forward.

Soon there are enough drops in the bucket to make a visible rising of the water level. And the amount of drop continues to double. Then the bucket appears to be filling. Not long after, the water seems about ready to spill over the edge.

That, friends, is exactly the state of your consciousness bucket at this time. And the drops keep multiplying. Or to use another analogy that you are fond of, you are the ninety-ninth monkey.

Now it is not necessary for you to find the last monkey, the one hundredth monkey. As a matter of fact, what follows will be one hundred and ninety-eight monkeys, right? All that you need do is take care of your own consciousness and watch the fun.

The spill over the sides of the bucket has begun. Watch. Observe. Enjoy. Make it your intent to see the positive side of what is happening around you. See the changes as what is needed to produce the next higher condition. We promise you, not long from now, many will look back and say, "What happened?" Be the water drop that knows. And yes, we know we have hopelessly mixed our metaphors. Enjoy that, too.

We wish to revisit today our past discussions of a topic. We have spoken often of your consciousness. Today we would introduce a few ways of viewing this extremely important subject that you have perhaps not considered before.

As has been said before, the beginning may be a good place to start. Let's begin with everything that exists. Everything that exists is energy, is frequency. All energy is conscious. It contains information. It creates. You have various terms and understandings for this. You tend to believe that your term and understanding must be the only correct one, but that is another topic. You also tend to personify this Source. That is also another discussion in itself.

Have you taken the next obvious step in your thinking? If it is all energy, and it is all conscious, then everything you can see around you is to some degree conscious. All-That-Is is conscious. That is. Therefore, that is conscious.

We have previously told this channel that there are further things that can be intuited from this. For instance, if everything is one field of consciousness, including oneself, and if one is unaware of what is being held in the consciousness of what one is looking at, then what one is looking at is in what you term your subconscious. Also, consider that if it is in the conscious field but unknown to your awareness, then it is possible for you to become aware of it.

Does this not open up a whole new universe of possibilities to you? All of the things that you considered impossible, or possible only to others, beyond your capability and 'magical' just become as normal as walking and talking when you view your mind in this way.

Now everyone is not a mechanic, or a physicist, or a mathematician. Neither will everyone express themselves in the same ways in conscious abilities of perception and communication. Nor will everyone be moving things around with only their will and focus. But this is not for lack of capability so much as differences in need, experience, and focus. Farmers have little need of string theory, do you see? But physicists do not usually know much about soil composition either. So on another note, please do not continue to judge one as being above another. Both are needed.

So, back to our subject; look around you right now, and realize that everything you are seeing is conscious energy expressing itself temporarily as the things you are looking at. It is solid, if that is what you are looking at, because you perceive it as solid. You are solid because you agree to be solid. And no, we are not saying that you can terminate that agreement abruptly. So please continue to be solid for the moment. But we hope to be giving you entirely new things to consider regarding your 'reality'. Reality is what it is, yes. But perhaps your human understandings of what that is are not as accurate as you think.

Now consider this. To some extent, your perceptions influence the entire world around you. You may understand that you influence your immediate surroundings far more than what is far removed from you. But that also means that your ability to change what is in your life at a particular time is something that you can have an effect upon.

It means you are not a helpless victim of circumstance. Of course, if you feel the need to be a helpless victim, you are free to do so. But in taking ownership of the power of your thoughts and feelings to influence your world, you will begin to learn who you are. You will begin to understand why you are. You will begin to see what your place is meant to be in this 'grand scheme of things' that you love to make reference to.

There are many things that you frequently express the desire to have and to do. But we wish to tell you this day that until you claim for yourself that you are the one whom we tell you that you are, you will not find within yourself the power to have and to do those things. You have been carefully taught that those abilities are not human abilities. We tell you that they certainly are.

Many consider these things to be divine in nature. And we say that you are correct. And you may claim them. And since you are now thinking in new ways, what does that mean? Who are you?

What, after all, does the word ascension mean to you? Ponder that. What does it mean and why would it be possible? And it is possible! Go for it. We're saving you a seat.

It Rings True

Purpose and Path

We have determined that it is now time to explore for and with you, as you read or hear this message, your purpose and chosen journey from this Council to your current incarnate state. You often hear this mentioned in one way or another, but seldom do many of you allow yourselves to truly understand the magnitude of the thing you have chosen to do. After all, you are just another in a long line of billions of personalities in body on your beautiful blue orb, are you not? Well, no. You are not. But also, yes, you are. It is the amazing value and worth of this that we would discuss today.

Firstly, whether you believe in the fact that most of you are there for your most recent of a great many incarnations or not, the fact is that you are the latest in a long, long line of 'you' that has been a part of all that has gone into becoming what humanity is. All of your 'bad' lives, and all of your so-so lives, and all of your brilliant lives are what has gone into making up who you are as individuals and who you are as the being called humanity. And yes, we did say the being, singular, called humanity. Because each level of consciousness, from the inception of a thought to its ultimate potential, is a being. Let's stick with you, however.

It has all been, and is, and will be experience, a learning experience. It is the experience of I AM learning who I AM can be.

Now, it is not the first time anyone has told you that a short time ago, about 70 years, it became obvious that your planet needed help if she was going to survive with you still on board. And since that time, members of this consciousness have asked to be allowed to return, and in some cases, go for the first time, to earth in order to participate in this grand shift and ascension into a higher state of being than that which had evolved there up to that point. When we say members of this consciousness, we mean to tell you that you are members in good standing of these Councils.

We think it is time for you to begin understanding and learning to live as the invaluable, magnificent creator beings that you are. And unless you can allow for the possibility that that is truly who you are and may be, you cannot manifest as that, do you see?

Perhaps you need only to be able to see the immeasurable value of what it is that you are already doing on your journeys. You have taken a facet of the light that we all are, and you have, against all odds, brought it into the denser vibrations of your reality and held it there as more and more arrived to raise the entire consciousness of mankind. This is no small feat! This is universe changing! And it is almost to the point now that your success will become obvious to all who have eyes to see.

We want you to have eyes to see. Humility is a virtue; however, self-worth and the ability to know who and what you are is also a virtue. We are not speaking of over inflated egos. We are speaking of not denigrating who you are, what Creator has made you. Take joy from the knowing. Take strength from the knowing when you need it. We are well aware, even those of us who have not been where you are, that immense strength is often necessary to do what you are doing. Is it any wonder then that we often speak of our respect and admiration for you?

Have this respect for yourselves, and in that realization, have respect for all those around you who are having just as rough a time of it as you are, even if it appears to be otherwise from your viewpoint. All have their own battles to wage. All are climbing the same mountain.

We await your return to us with open arms and great love. Good day.

Why are you here? What are you here for? What should you be doing?

These are the questions you always, always ask us. Do you ask because you are truly lost? No. You ask because, deep in your heart, you know. You know that you came here for a reason.

"But I don't know the reason" you say. Well, actually you do. And what is popping up before you in your life is what you have decided to work on. It is there for one or more of several possible reasons. It may be the principle reason for your being here. It may be something that you have agreed to clear before you begin working on your principal goal. It may something you have agreed to work on for mankind's benefit. It may include aspects of all of these.

The one thing that is invariably true is that it will continue to appear before you in various guises until you have handled it. It is also true that once you have awakened to your purpose, agreed to do what is before you today, and simply set out to move forward on this path, you will discover that it gives you a happy feeling of satisfaction. You begin to draw into your life things that bring you more and more joy and satisfaction. You begin to see possibilities that never occurred to you before.

So here is the apparently 'hidden' truth. Your path, that elusive thing that you have searched and searched for, is the path you are on. It is only hidden because you have hidden it. And you have hidden it so that you could 'find' it. There is an aspect of you, the very largest part of who you are, that never forgets, that never doesn't know, and that always works with us to see that you are exactly where you need to be, for yourself and for the ALL. And you have a self-correcting guidance system. Did you know that?

Your guidance system is not in your pocket, and you can't leave home without it. Most of you still don't know about it, or know about it and forget to use it all too often. We tell you this over and over again. We tell you many things over and over again. We find infinite ways to dress up simple truths in order to keep you on track and to inform those of you who are just awakening. That's our job. So where is this guidance system?

It's in your heart. That is not news, is it? News flash! Just do what feels good and right for you. Notice we did not say to do what anyone else says is right for you. We did not say to find it in a book. You will know because you know. You will know because you know. You will know because you know. But you will not know if you do not value what you know. You will not know if you doubt what you know. You will not know if you do not listen to what you know.

So what to do now? We suggest that you may want to begin with a game of 'what if?' What if all of the things that councils and guides and angels and teachers have been telling me over and over are true? What if I really am a divine being? What if I really do know? What if I really can? What if I always have been? What if the time really is now? What will I do today if I know it really will matter?

Because, dearest friend, they are, you are, you do, you can, and you always have. It is. And we promise you, what you do really does matter. You can suffer this, or you can have fun with that. You choose. That's another thing that is unavoidably true. You choose. Spend some time watching a toddler choose. Then go out and have fun with that. Because you can. Good day.

We shall speak now of dedication. You quite likely have not thought of yourself as being dedicated, yet almost all of you are dedicated to something. Give this a moment's thought. What are you dedicated to?

Are you dedicated to things that reflect the nature of your being? And the answer to that is, yes. Of course you are. Now, list what those things are. You will find a very accurate description of what the current state of your consciousness is. We suggest that this might be very useful. This is a mirror, you see.

What we are attempting to give you is an awareness of things that you can sort through and keep, enhance, or discard. Are you dedicated to family? Hmmm, that's a keeper. Are you dedicated to your work? If so, why? We hope you can see that this could be either a beneficial or a harmful sort of dedication.

Make this list be as long as you are able. These are things that you put your energy into. Your energy is the most valuable thing you have. It is your power. It is what you are. As you learn to see where you best apply it, it can turn into an extremely powerful force in your life.

Of course, it is already powerful, but are you using it to your most beneficial effect? Is it being focused on getting you where you want to go, wherever that may be? We are not judging that. You are the one who is free to choose.

We would point out to you that it would be of the most benefit to you if the choice were made consciously. Awareness of what you do and why you choose to do it is a large part of what you are calling being awake. It is not only the awareness of what is going on around you. That is important. But the awareness that brings your own growth is the truly powerful awareness. That is what will change you. And that change is what will ultimately change everything.

While we are at it, let us also point out that you cannot be increasing this awareness purposefully without being "in the now." And now is a good time for you to be in.

Also, "I am _____.", "I dedicate myself to _____.", and "I choose to _____" are power statements. These are thoughts that recover your power. Realize the divine, powerful being that you are. Choose what you will do with that. Instead of asking why you are here, create why you are here. That is your true power. Good day.

The most common, no, the universal question asked of us and of guides on both sides of the veil is, "Am I on the right path?" The second is, "What should I be doing?" May we spend a bit of time with you today and clear that up?

There are many things we can bring into this discussion. We could answer the entire thing with the simple words of the source you call Abraham. "You cannot ever finish it, and you cannot get it wrong." However, let's give it a bit more discussion than that, shall we?

First, we will point out that you are there as a representative facet of the being who sat, and continues to sit, in conference with a council of guides, teachers, masters, and soul family who determined, and continue to determine, the why and how of your present incarnation. By far the greater part of the being you indeed are is not the tiny physical body and limited mind that you think you are. You are growing into the realization of that. It is, in fact, a large part of your purpose to do so.

You have a purpose for being where you are. You do not, most of you, remember what that is. And to most of you it remains a mystery because you do not think that you have access to the greater part of you, or you do not even suspect that there is a greater part of you. Well there is. And it is becoming known more and more widely as the spiritual side of humankind comes more to the forefront.

Even though each of you must begin this journey from where he or she finds themselves, you are all on that path. Where you stand is on that path. Your next step will be on that path. You cannot be anywhere else. It would serve you not at all to be on another's path.

What should you be doing? You should be doing what you do best and feel the best about doing. You've been taught that if you are having fun, you cannot be doing the best thing. You've been taught that because there are those that wanted you to do what they expected of you. The fact is that the feelings of joy and accomplishment, the feelings of satisfaction, are the way that your Self, capital S, gets its guidance to you.

Now, if you have been following closely, you know that there are other ways, as well. As we said above, you are a part of this Council. You are continually guided, counseled, and taught by whomever has the guidance and information that you need. That is one of the reasons that you need sleep, you know. And that is why you are so frequently told you should spend time in nature, meditate, etc.

Some of you come away with visions, with memories, with words of wisdom ringing in your heads. Some of you think that you get nothing. Let us assure you that if you make the effort, the effort is never wasted. But if you are one who learns best in one way, do not expect to be taught another way. Actually, the very most effective thing for you to do is to spend time with your awareness centered in your feelings and just stop thinking in the past (judgment) or the future (worry). You can do that anywhere, but the peace of nature, a park, a garden, where life is only concerned with living, and the peace of that is pervasive, will certainly make you feel better in short order.

Now, remember we said that you cannot get it wrong? That is true because you and the universe will always learn something. You true question is, "What will get me what I think I want in the quickest way?" Is that not accurate? Also, "How can I keep from making a huge mistake?" One answer to that is above. Another is that you will receive what you need.

But we will offer this: you cannot go wrong if you stay in appreciation and thanks for what you have and what you receive.

Now, you may think, "I can't just drop everything and run off and become a (fill in the blank). I have obligations. I have to eat." Can you do it for a few minutes? Can you learn something more about it? Can you watch someone do it? You get the idea. We would say that is the next step on your path that you 'should' take. Please notice that we put the word should in quotes. What we mean is that you may find it to be beneficial to your learning and growth. And you may also find that it is a gift you can share with the world.

There is nothing that you can contribute to the world more helpful than the keeping of yourself in a higher vibration. That means, oddly enough, that it is very helpful for you to be happy. And happy is something you can be if you decide to be. It is a thing that you can do. Do that. Do it a lot. Make it a habit. Make it be what people think of when they think of you.

Forgiveness

There is one overriding thing that must be addressed by each and all of you. It is a problem that none of you are exempt from unless and until you have completed the path which you currently term ascension. It would be the grand finale of our messages, but instead of a grand finale, let us get to it now and let you understand that everything else leads to this, and you have the need to address it continually until it is truly completed.

What we are speaking of is the need for you to forgive. You need to forgive others. You need to forgive whomever you understand as the Supreme Being. And lastly, but most importantly, you need to forgive yourself.

Now, forgiving others, you surely understand. Although you have judged them, you therefore find that almost impossible to do, in many cases. And we may as well address that now. Stop. What you are doing is projecting things that you deem less than desirable onto others, assuming your assessment of them to be correct, and then allowing yourself to think less of them because of it. There is more to it than that, of course, but that explanation is enough to show you that what you are doing is actually harmful to yourself. Taken to the perspective of the ALL, you are, in fact, judging The One of which you are a part, as is the other whom you judge.

Please understand the same is true when you judge yourself. You are withholding love from yourself. You are withholding forgiveness from yourself. And your Self is an integral part of the ALL. Also, you are, in effect, saying that your Creator has made an awful mistake in creating you. Well, that is not the case.

As for forgiving the Supreme Being, whatever you have been taught to call that, you have all been taught over many lifetimes that an all-powerful being will judge you and punish you for thoughts, deeds, and words. You are afraid of that being even as you tell yourself that She loves you. Is that not so? There is a huge conflict in beliefs contained in that. God is Love. He will send me to suffer forever for what I have done or not done. Well this is just not so, and the reasoning behind that we can discuss at length at another time. But you may wish to forgive that being for what you have erroneously believed Her to be. You will find your load much easier to bear.

Now we can offer you a way to stop incurring the drawbacks of judgment if you like. It is necessary for you to learn what is desirable and what is not. And no one is telling you that it is desirable to rape, kill, pillage, steal, cheat, etc., etc.

But it is one thing to recognize that an action is undesirable, and it is quite another to condemn the one who does it. All you need to do is to stop judging beings. Your Creator does not.

Is this enough for you to mull over for today? We think it is. If it is, we invite you back to read the next message, which will be about why these resonate with you, if they do, and what that may lead you to.

Be at peace within yourselves, dear friends. You are not broken. You do not need fixing. And you are loved.

Our message today will concern forgiveness. Once again we are speaking of something that is not new to most of you; however, it is an important thing for you to consider at this time.

You may think that you have spent more than enough time on this in past meditations, past healing practices, past inner explorations. And for a great many of you, it is true that you have been very conscientious regarding the forgiveness of others. Some have even worked quite a bit on forgiving themselves. Some have understood the necessity of digging out their resentments toward the universe and even divinity itself for past situations. And these are all commendable. However, it is now time to revisit the whole concept.

Why is that? Well, it is because you have done so well. It is precisely because you have come so far that there is now before you the opportunity to make a final push into the next level consciousness. And so now you are being presented with the rising into your dreams and meditations things with which you thought you were finished. "What is this?" you think. "I finished this years ago!"

Please do not be upset with yourselves over this. We could go into a long dissertation about the cyclical nature of time. We could do the 'peeling the onion' thing. And, yes, there are those who are still in much earlier stages of this sort of clearing and forgiveness. So, whatever method you know or can find for clearing these things, do that. If, however, you are one of those whom we described above, and you have devoted long years to clearing yourself, be aware that it is possible that only the smallest traces of these things may remain in your consciousness to be finally cleared. You may only need to look directly at what is presented to you, recognize it, and allow it to go on its way. Send it back to the light to be transformed. "I am not this. I do not engage with this. I am now done with these things."

It is a wonderful thing that so many of you are now in a place that allows us to bring you such a message. The momentum you have achieved is nothing short of remarkable. You may think accurately of it as escape velocity. Please don't imagine this to mean you are leaving you sweet planet. But you are certainly ready to leave the negativity behind. You are more than ready, we think, to spend much more of your time finding and celebrating the beauty around you. See it everywhere. See it even more in those places where it seems to be well hidden. Uncover it. Restore it. It is time to begin the task of recreating beauty in your world. As always, it will come from within. As always, no one can do it where you are better than you can. Be our hands. Be our feet. Feel our love, our presence, and our joy.

It Rings True

Freedom and Free Will

We would speak with you today about a topic that we have not addressed in this space previously. We are very hopeful that many of you will be helped by what we share with you

We know that there are still quite a large number of those who consider themselves to be lightworkers and star seeds who think of themselves as being alone, cut off, separated from any contact with like minds for conversation and companionship. Let us address this topic in a way that may help you to change this perception and remedy the situation.

We do wish to make clear that at least in the vast majority of cases, this is a perception, and not necessarily an accurate one. And even if accurate, it is easily one that can be remedied by lightworkers, both because they have the ability as lightworkers to do so, and because the time has arrived, and the energy environment exists for all of you to become aware of one another.

Let us speak of your perception of isolation first. It is very likely only a perception. Please understand that. Now the reasons for that perception vary widely. And yet there is a sameness about them, as well. We are, in a way, sorry to inform you that you are protecting yourselves from what you expect to be less than friendly acceptance of your views by those around you. And it is possible that you might well experience some of that. But we ask you now several questions.

Except for a few isolated pockets in the world, are you aware that you will not be attacked or killed for your views? You are holding onto fears that you carry from many past experiences. They were valid at one time. They do not serve you now.

Do you not realize that, with the number of you now spread across this planet, the likelihood that you are truly isolated, wherever you are, is remote? You are still somewhat of a minority, yes. But there are quite likely others close to you who are protecting themselves, just as you are. And they feel isolated, too.

And lastly, do you not think that by refusing to hide yourself away any longer you will attract each other, that the feeling of freedom you experience will be worth any amount of sideways glances from others, and that the power of united minds and hearts will not be immense?

Of course, you know that is true. And you only needed reminding. Let us tell you today that it is time now. You are needed now. And you will be appreciated now. Stand up. Stand your ground. Be the truth of yourselves. Perhaps cease to be a lightworker. Be a light warrior.

We are with you. Always and in all ways, we are with you. Love to you this day.

Today let's look at the subject of freedom. To many that seems to mean that they are able to do anything that they wish. Most adults understand it to mean something with a bit more responsibility than that. But what does it truly mean, and do you experience it?

We would like to suggest to you that freedom might actually mean that you are able to do anything that your heart desires within the restraints of the universal laws of the universe in which you are participating. You are also free to experience what it is like to work against those laws, but you just might find that to be a mite uncomfortable.

Usually, however, you interpret it to mean something quite a bit closer to home, like your day-to-day lives in your societies. And again, we ask you, are you free? Do you feel no restrictions upon your activities? If so, wonderful for you! You are quite unique. If not, what is restricting you?

Much of what you find, when you examine this, will have its source in collective consciousness. Some of it will be due to things you have been told and have accepted. Some will be due to things you believe about yourselves. Almost all of it will be things that you may never have considered questioning.

Now we are not suggesting that you begin violating society's rules willy-nilly. Anarchy is not our agenda. What we do suggest is that you examine those things that you consider impossible for you, for those are things to which you have released your personal power. Do you agree to that or do you not? If you do consciously agree, and that is not automatically a negative thing, then so be it. If you decide to take your power back, then at least consider the possibility that it could be within your capability. Just claim it. Know that it is something within your potential.

Now we can tell you that there isn't anything that doesn't fit into that category, but what we are intending here is that you begin a process of expanding your own personal freedom to choose. Just begin. The process will continue. "I am much more than I have ever thought myself to be." Amaze yourself.

Now, for extra credit, as you would say, here is something that will accelerate you on this path. Consider that if this is true for you, it is also true for all those next to you. They are, indeed, much more than you have ever thought them to be. When you can see them in that light, your world will change. And we mean that quite literally. Inside that one whom you do not like the looks of or whose actions you are opposed to is a spark of divinity just as powerful as that spark within you. It is not necessary for you to agree with what they do or say. But learn to live in a world where they are free to think or say it. Live in a world where what is inside of them is important and how they appear is not. They are here to learn, just as you are. And it is quite possible that they have chosen to learn some very hard lessons. We promise you that you have done the same many times in the past. Seeing them for the divine sparks that they are and allowing them the freedom to learn their lessons in their own way will also allow them the freedom to change. Attempting to change them will almost never work, however.

What will work is living your own life as a totally loving being. Imagine a world where billions of you did only that. Perhaps things might change? Just be the one who holds love where you are. Many are joining this practice daily. This is something that is happening. It is not a pipe dream. You only need do your part.

With great love we send our blessings. Good day.

Today we would like to discuss the subject of your freedom. There is much available on this topic now, and most of it is a conversation you are having among yourselves that involves political and societal issues. This is not what we wish to explore with you. The freedom we wish to talk about is of a different nature.

We have spoken with you of judgments that you have made and continue to make about yourselves. We have spoken to you of the judgments that you continue to believe that Creator has made of you and your actions, thoughts and words. We have spoken with you of the limitations that you have placed upon yourselves as well as the ones that you have accepted because you have been told you have them. There are even ones that you have inferred from your experiences. These include, also, things that have been brought into this life from previous lifetimes, from the lives and experiences of your lineage through your DNA, and in some cases, things that you have agreed to overcome to the benefit of mankind even though they are not your own issues at all. This seems like what could be quite a mountain for you to move, doesn't it?

Let us ask you to consider first the ways that you prolong and continue the condition, the seeming prison, in which you find yourselves. Think of the way you give away your power to change when you think or say I wish, I pray, I try, or I hope. What could you have said or thought that would assume for you the power to change. We urge you to use I can, I am, I do, and anything else that shows that *you* are the deciding force in your own life. And then there is the law of assumption, if we may call it that. When you live in an attitude of gratitude for the accomplishment of your change, when you think and say thank you in your every hour of every day, you will find that you move that mountain easily. At first it may budge, then it might slide, but sooner than you think possible, it will just seemingly decompose, cease to exist.

All is energy, after all. And when you change the energy, you change the all. These two concepts are things that we constantly repeat. First, all is energy. Second, you create and change the all. That is what is meant by co-creation. And you will spend your eternity learning exactly what that can mean. But for now, begin to learn what it can mean on this plane. It is a gift that we dearly wish for you to begin using. It is a major aspect of the 'image' that you were created in.

Now, this has been a somewhat weighty discussion today, and you know that often we try to keep things a bit lighter. So we wish you an enjoyable and happy time until we speak with you again. Good day.

We wish to explain a bit about free will, if we may. There is a view that, since your ultimate destination is decreed by Creator to be oneness, there is no free will. There is also a view that it means one can do whatever one pleases in the moment.

Both are true in that your ultimate destination is oneness with Creator, and you are able to act in complete disregard for the consequences. In the first instance, you will make vast amounts of decisions between here and there. In the second, you just may find that there are, indeed, consequences—some good, some not so wonderful.

Also, be aware that your oneness will not entail the loss of knowing all that you have learned and experienced. What would be the point of that?

Do you see that all of the above describes differing levels of lesson learning? If one ignores one's knowing and guidance too long, one gets to learn what you call hard lessons. And the results of the decisions one makes, or avoids making, also lead to learning. Whether one considers those lessons good or bad is purely subjective, and from the viewpoint of having lived your life, you will look back and literally say, "It's all good." Is it not a good thing to know that stovetops are hot?

Some say that Divine Will rules all, and that means you do not truly have free will. We will explain it in this manner: when you are truly in alignment with your true Divine Self, your will **is** Divine Will. The apparent difference is only apparent because you consider yourself to be in separation, and this is illusion. As you are often being told, you cannot and do not exist in separation from Creator. This is also said as "God is All", etc. And this is quite literally true. It is even good logic. God is All That Is. You are made from what is. You are, therefore, an integral part of God.

Now, since that is undeniably true, does it not seem evident that your will is also a part of Divine Will? Do not confuse willfulness with the will we are speaking of. Common sense may not be all that common, but it remains that your inner knowing, that knowing that is guided by what is best for you and for all others, will not lead you astray.

These are things you know. Things ring true, if they ring true, because they are things that you know. And if a thing fits into that category, it will never be new. It will be universal and eternal. Occasionally, however, we may do a bit of reminding.

So freely exercise your free will. It is one of the things you are here to do. You will notice that we in council, in guidance, in service, do not ever tell you what you must do. We are in service to your lives. We advise, we chide, we prod. Sometimes we get pretty adamant. But the decisions in your lives must be your own. That is where the learning occurs. And every experience produces learning; so don't worry so much about whether you are doing it wrong. It is understood that you do the best you know how. Your perseverance is of great wonder to us.

Many here have been there. It takes input from experience to understand what you are living. We do appreciate your circumstances. Yet we may only aid you in your chosen lessons. There will come a time when you look back and give thanks for that. And we do hear a few saying "Yeah, right!" to that. But we also know you will always keep on keeping on.

Blessings to all who read this. Our unconditional love is yours. You are exactly where you need to be. Good day.

The Flow

We have told you before, more than once, that you were in the thick of the changes, the awakening, the increasing light and energy. Still, many continued to say that nothing was happening. Many will still say that, as their focus is not on their internal life, but on the external. Let us confirm for those in the forefront now, however, that just as they are beginning to suspect, their own evolution of being, of consciousness, is now in full force. Abilities are coming online. Plans are changing. Opportunities are not only knocking but are, in many cases, leading you by the nose. Things you always dreamed of but were considered 'impossible' are becoming your reality.

We want to give you a picture now of the best way to handle this if, indeed, you see that we are describing your current life events. You have heard of the flow. You are familiar with the 'vortex'. We have used the image of waterfalls. All of those ideas picture what this is going to continue to be like. In fact, it will only increase. You have become so good at surfing this wave, however, that you may be experiencing this as a smoothing ride now. And in fact, the largest and most uncomfortable of the changes are over for most of you. Now the 'good stuff' will begin to unfold.

There will still be an occasional bump in the road. That is called life. But in order to move that around the bend for yourself, we ask you to surrender. That word troubles many of you, but you interpret our meaning incorrectly. We mean for you to push off into mid-stream and allow the current to carry you. And we do not wish to give the image of an uncontrollable current, but of a huge inner power, a power that is you.

We have taken great pains to get you to understand that whatever you have been used to seeing as external force is actually power intrinsic to yourselves. It is not that the power you observe outside you is not there, but that it is also your power. You are a part of it. You are beginning to understand that, and as you do, you learn how to use it. We have called this an "E ticket ride". Have fun! Please keep your arms and legs inside the vehicle at all times.

One last thought. As your newfound abilities begin to surface, and even the most able of you will have some, please do not forget to develop control of these, as well. As an example, if you become able to hear things you have not heard before, be sure you learn to turn it down or off when you require it. Do not be overwhelmed by it. This is also true of all the rest. You have filtered these things out of your consciousness for quite a long time, and they will take some getting used to.

Blessings of love and light to each of you this day.

Many of you are going through what seems to you to be a rather bumpy period at this time. You are thinking, "What are they blathering about... a great leap toward a new way of being? I haven't had a great leap! If anything, this is worse." As we mentioned before, remember that there is a part of you that sees around corners and over obstacles. Unfortunately for your conscious mind, most of you do not have constant access to this when you are dealing with your physical surroundings.

If there is anything that is in your way, anything that is slowing down your progress now, it is imperative, given your intention to make said progress, that you toss it overboard or resolve it before you move on. You aren't going to get very much further upon the path you have set for yourself without doing this. And if you try, you know how it will go. The further you travel without the resolution, the more difficult the resolution will seem. As an example of this, think of the times that it takes humans to manifest a grave illness before they start to look for answers. Is it not the case that many, many opportunities were missed?

Another possible sort of problem you may encounter is the holding onto something that you will need to let go of. You may be being presented with an opportunity that you do not recognize. You may be being shown that you are identifying yourself with yet one more thing that you, in fact, are not. Allow us to point out to you something that you are already very well aware of but are possibly overlooking in your focus upon what you are interpreting as a problem.

There is absolutely nothing that you are experiencing, or having, or wanting to maintain a hold upon, which is not temporary. Being temporary is what is meant by the term illusion. The only, stress that, *the only,* thing that you are aware of in your 'reality' that is, in fact, permanent and therefore real, is yourself. Actually, let's make that your Self. Everything else is illusory, and therefore, can never be held on to. It will change. And the attempt to stop or slow that change is the cause of much, much suffering on your parts.

So, what do you do about that? That has not changed either. And most of you would know exactly what to advise another who asked you that question. If you were asked about a thing or situation, you would most likely respond by saying, "Release it." You might say, "Look for ways to turn it into a winning situation for everyone." In any case, you would know to throw massive amounts of love at it. You would know to release all of your expectations, all of your doubts, and all of your fearful thinking about it.

This is the key after all, is it not? Are you not most likely holding onto the past because you cannot see the future and are not confident of what it might be?

Now, we cannot show you the future. Because the future is so far removed from what you know, any imagined picture that we could send you would need to be based in images that you know now. And do you know what? That wouldn't even begin to do it justice. So that is why we are always using flowery descriptions of things "beyond your imagination", because it is beyond your imagination. But along the way, there are steps you will need to take that are easily imagined if you let go and allow the next necessary steps to take place. Your life will only hold so much. You want or need more. Does not something have to go? Kiss your old car good-bye, thank it for its service, and go car shopping with a free and open heart. Car, job, relationship, or anything else, the same principles apply. And you know this. That is why you love the phrase "Go with the flow" so much.

Now, breathe and make that leap forward we spoke of. You are loved and supported.

It Rings True

What Is Happening

If you could see what is happening to so many others at this time as we do, you would have a much clearer and more optimistic view of your circumstances than most of you do. You see, clearly or not so clearly, your own progress. You know of what may be happening for friends and acquaintances, perhaps. Even at that, your knowledge is limited to what you are told and your own interpretations of it.

We, however, see the entire tapestry of your collective. How could we not, since we, as we have been at pains to teach you, are deeply involved as participants in the entire process. It is also important for you to begin to understand the fact that you are also completely involved. That is a large part of what you will begin to understand now with the lifting of the veil, the parting of the curtain.

We will paint for you now a quick picture, if you will, of a very important process that is currently going on for many. You have seen it mentioned here and in other places, but you may have given it less attention than it warrants. In no way do we wish you to feel left out if the specific things we mention are not a part of your current experience. What we wish to do is alert you to watch your own inner selves and outer lives for like changes. Some are receiving the activation of abilities that they did not know they would have. Some are having meetings, in dream state or out, with beings other than those they thought possible. Some have sat in a moment of wonder upon realizing that certain things have ceased to 'push their buttons', as you say. And some are able to understand that they are experiencing a merging with higher aspects of self. And there are many, many more things that we do not mention.

There are around seven billion of you there, each one unique in make-up and purpose. We do not have that much space here. So let us point out that what you most need to ready yourselves for, and what is to come next, is what you and we are bringing about for you now.

Some will not choose to receive it. But those who follow these types of message will be either kicking-and-screaming or sliding-and-laughing receivers. You have so chosen, and you will NOT be left behind.

Now, it is time to surrender. OH, you do not like that word. And we understand why that is. What we are asking you to do, however, is to let us have the reins for a bit and to hang on to your saddles for dear life for the next short while.

Consider it a carnival ride. Or, as your humorists would say, "Hold my beer and watch this!"

This, dear ones, is going to be a fun year if you treat it that way. Of course there are things to be straightened out, which may not appear very pretty at the time, but keep your focus and all will be well.

With love we say, "Till next time."

We have come to the time for many of you. You feel it. Some of you hear it. You may feel some confusion. You may wonder why you now feel a bit at sea, cut loose, unable to see what lies ahead. You were so sure you knew and now do not. Let us give you an image that may help you understand what is happening.

You have been drifting faster and faster with the flow of inner change, drifting on a rising current. You have survived the occasional whitewater. Now there are those of you who have taken the lead, the forefront, who have reached the first cataract on your journey. You are over the edge and feeling as if in freefall. We hasten to tell you that everything is still proceeding well for you. Do not worry. This is a temporary feeling.

You have been swept by your momentum into new territory for you. And this is a good thing. It will take a short while of trusting the process, trusting your guides, trusting your Higher Selves. But, as always, you will soon get your bearings and find that you are exactly where you should be, though some might find themselves in unexpected surroundings, so to speak.

Please realize that quite often, the results of your efforts are better than you can imagine if you do not insist on exactly what you ask for and nothing else. Your conscious mind can only extrapolate from what it remembers. Very rarely can you dream in quantum jumps from what you know. And quantum jumps are what some of you are engaged in now.

Some of you have asked to take on even more than you originally contracted for this time around. You were anticipating so well that you shrugged and thought you may as well buy the "E ticket ride." So, as we have urged you often before, buckle your seatbelts and hang on. You are being made ready for what you asked for... or something better.

We love you. Enjoy the ride. We will speak again soon.

As you go through your day, are you finding that you are reacting to situations that used to 'push your buttons' in ways that surprise you? Have you changed so much? Are you one of those who is experiencing unexplainable things around you? Are you seeing things that you were never able to see before? Perhaps you even question whether or not you really did see them? Hearing things? Knowing things you never knew and don't know how you know? Are you having dreams that are much clearer and more promising? Are you feeling as if something huge and important is just around the next corner?

Welcome to March of this new year. Welcome to the new you. For those of you on the top end of your planet, spring is about to spring. For **all** of you, your spring is beginning to bloom. We have told you many times that you each have remarkable gifts which you have brought with you for this new time. Many of you have wondered what we were speaking of. If, and as, you search inside for your true selves, you will now find these things. Some will not seem so very impressive to you. Let us assure you that you have exactly what is needed for where you are.

At first, you may feel a bit at sea as you step into the new. This is not unusual, is it? It is the same as learning anything new. You may be impressed with what you are learning. It is only the beginning. Those who are stepping into roles as way showers have done this more times than you could count. It may be tempting to doubt your ability. Instead, we suggest you look inside and find your worth. We have discussed this many times.

You probably have grown tired of hearing how you were the strongest and the best. If you had any conscious awareness of what is at stake, you would never expect that anyone less would be trusted with this assignment. Mankind is about to wake up and look around. He may rub his eyes and stumble to the shower. He may have to stretch a few times. But, oh, what a day he has ahead of him. And most of you will have a ringside seat.

Remember to see everything as a part of the wonderful changes, no matter how they are portrayed in your media. At first, you will be told the sky is falling. When it doesn't fall, things may become just a bit clearer to those who can understand what is happening. That would be you. Resist the urge to say, "I told you so." Just help where help is asked for. Just be peaceful. Joyful will be all right, too.

Blessings, dear friends. As always, feel our presence and our love.

This is the time of the avalanche, the waterfall, and the immensely heightened frequency that we have spoken of so often before. It will continue to increase, but you already are into rates of change that you are struggling to deal with. This is as it was forecast, and it is necessary. You will make it. Set your minds at ease in that regard. It is being closely monitored and gauged individually. If you are indeed in overwhelm, it is time to stop and breathe. And you may ask for our help. You know this.

There are a great many reasons for what is happening and for the ramping up of which we speak, not the least of which is that it is making the perception of it unavoidable for more and more of you. There is a great awakening happening now.

There are those reading this who began their awakening years ago. There are also those who are still trying to piece together an understanding of the situation and are finding it very difficult to do while this whirlwind of change becomes more and more manifest into the physical world that you seem to be living in. It is a world that is reflecting the vast change in consciousness you have undergone and are yet experiencing. In other words, you are successfully doing what you are there to do.

And that brings us to the point of today's message. We would title this "Doors Are Opening" if it needed a title. You are increasingly bringing to yourselves the people, resources, and experiences that you need to accomplish your life purpose. You say, "But I don't know what that is!" And we answer, "Yes, you do." The evidence that the major part of you that is awake and aware knows exactly what he or she needs to do is all around you. It is only the remnant of your consciousness that still considers itself to be separate from us, from the All, that does not know that it knows. In many respects, it is afraid to know.

It is afraid of a judgment that it still thinks may be in store for it (there is none). It is afraid of the responsibility that it will bring. The divine being that is the true you knows its worth and its power. It is never afraid. The small you is not in any danger in that regard. Allow that divine you to be incarnate. That is what the term ascension truly means. Breathe YOU into you. Breathe light into you. Discover how amazing you really are.

As you do this, the wonderful action of synchronicity will begin to surface more and more into your life. You will discover that as you move along the path, things just happen unexpectedly exactly as and when you need them. Your life can be truly joyful and amazing if you let it be. We are overusing that word amazing, yes? Well, life should be amazing where you are. If that were not possible, you would not be learning anything. Imagine yourselves where we are, meeting each other and telling your stories. "You won't believe this! I got down there and couldn't remember a THING! Man, what a mess I got into. THEN..."

So, as we were saying, doors are opening. You have waited a long time for this. Be prepared for a period of chaos. Not everyone is aware, as you know. And you may be a beacon, a guiding light. Do not attempt to be a savior. As you have very likely experienced, people who are not awake do not take well to being told what they must believe or think. Answer truthfully when asked, of course. But those who will come will have their own awakening as and when they are ready. That is what happened for you, is it not? That is a part of what this revving up is about, as we said. That will be one effect of the increasing chaos. All change contains an initial period of chaos. Else, why change? Do you think mankind normally considers changing when everything is wonderful? Why would they?

So allow yourselves to continue along your awakening paths. Allow yourselves to incorporate more and more of the higher consciousness that you are into your awareness. Find the wonder, the delight, and the joy in your lives. And flavor them with gratitude for it all. You still have a long way to go, but most of you who are reading this now know that you are on the way. And if we may be allowed our usual bit of lighthearted humor, we've got your back! So dance your dance and sing your song. It's time!

You seem to be having a rather difficult time getting into the channeling process for the last few days, and this is due to both the energetic climate and the unusual activity and focus during this time. We hear your requests for increasing clarity and skill in this process, and that also is having an effect. Things are in flux.

Keep working at this, and you will find the new processes easier and easier as you move along. Understand that, when processes are changing, it may often seem as if things have come to a standstill, even though the exact opposite is really the case. Include this last into the message that you publish, as many others will be noticing the same sort of seeming lull or blockage in their own processes.

Today we would discuss the continuing journey that you are all on at this time; specifically, the quantum leap forward that many of you are sensing is approaching. You can already begin to see the effects that the collective rise in your light signature is having on your outer world, and that will continue. But what you are now feeling is another milestone in your own development that will be enabled during this next alignment, or what you call gateway.

At first, it may seem very evident to many of you and then, as always, as you become used to the new energetic environment, it will become your normal. This is and has always been the way you perceive things. That is actually wonderful. It means that you have assimilated the changes and are able to operate well within the new energies.

This time, however, we would like for you to remember that, although things are now your new normal, they are quite different from all of the former normalcies that you have experienced, at least for quite a very long time. They are going to begin approaching what is *always* normal for you when you are not embodied in that density. You might also think of it as the density itself lightening, and you would not be that incorrect. It is also described by some of you as the lifting of the veil. That is true also, although it is more of a by-product than a description of the condition itself.

Now, what would we say about that? How would we advise you to approach this? Well, for those of you who are discovering new abilities and talents, we would say that you might want to play with them and not take them as things to pat your own backs about so much as things that you have always had and just discovered in your toy box.

For those of you who are discovering things that are a mite uncomfortable about yourselves, and this will be happening for some, we would have you know that this is just muddy water washing out of your hose and not anything to beat yourselves up over. Every one of you is standing in a different spot, so to speak, and everyone's next step will need to be what is needed for their own development. Rejoice and give thanks that you are seeing movement. You are not stuck, even though you are a bit impatient at times. You are moving forward far, far more rapidly than has even been possible for millennia, and yet you seem to see yourselves as 'stuck' quite a bit. It is rather humorous, really.

So, here you go, jumping into your futures without a parachute again. Have fun and know that you really are not without our constant support and loving help. One again, we wish to remind you to ask for help whenever and for whatever you need it. We are not too busy, and you are just as important as anyone else. Your concern over that possibility is admirable, but know that you have guides and angels whose only focus is on yourself. Ask. Always ask.

Once again, we will re-visit a subject we have spoken of before. We hear so many of you who are on your paths saying, "I'm stuck. Nothing is happening." And we are addressing this through many of our channels once again. In order to make sense of our answer, you will need to accept our interpretation of your circumstances, and this is usually something we do not like asking you to do. We would rather tell you to look around and reassess what you see. But in this case, there is yet not much for you to see. That is really what is causing your feeling. If you could see what we see, you would not feel the way that you do.

Regardless of what personal path you are living, your communal goals for this lifetime are those involving the ascension of yourselves and your planet and civilization. You will have feelings that involve your personal situation. You will also

151

have much more nebulous, but still powerful, feelings that relate to the current collective state of consciousness. That is, in fact, what you are experiencing at this time. And this begs the question, "What state of consciousness are you referring to?"

There are those who are telling you that you are standing upon the threshold of an immense change in almost every facet of your world. They are telling you that your own internal changes will be just as monumental. You have been told that the waiting has gone on long enough, and you have agreed with this. You have actually replied that you wish it to begin now. Well, my friends, you are about to get your wish.

You are in a time of releasing and clearing. You are in a time of rest. You are gathering yourselves for the great leap that approaches. We see it. You do not. If you did, you would be quite happy to have this period. The parts of you that are still on this side of the 'veil' understand. You should be aware by now that the parts of yourselves of which you are aware, at least for the greatest percentage of you, are actually only a very small part of your totality. Changing that is in great part what ascension is all about. And that is happening.

It is actually not possible for you to be 'stuck'. Nothing in creation is not undergoing some change at some rate. The only thing that never changes is change. Ironic isn't it?

In addition, we would say that there are, indeed, some of you that are experiencing periods of chaos as you prepare, as you clear the deck, so to speak. Just know that it is far better to do this now than when the real chaos starts.

And when that does indeed begin, please keep in mind that the huge shift you desire will not happen without some degree of what will appear to be total confusion. Venture past the building site of any new construction and try to envision the beautiful structure that the architect envisioned. What you see is great piles of materials that cannot be made sense of as they are lying about. But that beautiful building is there in its potentiality. That is where you are about to stand. And you will be doing the construction. Your dreams and intentions are the blueprints. Your lives will be the mortar and the nails. If you don't mind too much, we will kibitz and offer a bit of advice here and there.

Soon enough, you will have at least enough built for you to have an enjoyable world to live upon. We can promise that, because we see the finished product. Congratulations.

We are showing you a picture that includes images of several of what you call extreme sports. Many of you seem to enjoy having your adrenaline flood through you. Since you don't seem to have any saber toothed tigers to run from, you have taken to jumping from high places or plummeting down mountainsides.

When you stand upon that cliff or at the start of that ski run, you are very much in a place equivalent to humanity's position in its evolution at this time. The difference is that much of what you are now going to experience will seem to happen at a pace that will have you saying, as usual, "Nothing is happening". We have spoken of this before.

However, this will not always be the case. And for your screaming enjoyment, we offer you now the beginning of change that may have you breathless at times. Remember, you have asked for this; "bring it on" being one of your favorite phrases. You may use that less often in the future. But we are not wanting to frighten you at all. We actually want you to become excited at the possibilities that approach you now.

Begin now, if you will, to employ to even greater effect those tools you have that drive this change. These are your imagination, your intent, your focus, and your will. Everything else is driven by those things, just as it always has been.

As you see change occurring now, make it your practice to see the positive possibilities, even when others cry out the opposite. Keep always in your minds that new earth you have dreamed of. Be always more like the person you wish to be than you were yesterday. Drop your regrets and your judgments of self and hold only to your intentions. This is your power. Own it now.

We know you have felt lost and at a standstill for a little while now. Until your personal wild ride begins, take stock of yourselves and get ready. Be good scouts and be prepared. The fun will begin before too long.

Oh! And all that baggage you've been lugging around? Leave it there.

What in the world is going on?

Is that what you are feeling now? We know that many of you are. The more sensitive of you, even some who do not think of yourselves as such, are feeling, either physically, emotionally, or both, as if something immense that you just cannot describe is going on. Something is different. Are you going nuts? Even if you have felt this sort of thing for quite some time, this feels new. This feels different.

You are exactly correct. This is new. This is different. And yet this is what we have been talking to you about for three years or more. Three years seems like a long time to you. It is just another infinitely short period for us. In order to understand a lot of what we tell you, the concepts of "now time" and oneness are essential. Even then, a 3D mind just cannot truly know what we mean. But of course you will try. And of course, that is what you should do. That is how you are wired.

Think of these following things that we will list as all happening together for the first time: You are expanding your consciousness; your individual and collective frequencies are rising; earth's frequency signature has doubled and continues to rise; a very large number of other civilizations and spiritual beings are sending this planet as much light as they are able—much more than you can imagine; there are solar system alignments coming online that are contributing greatly; and there is now arriving, in your neighborhood, a wave of energy that, in your terms, headed in your direction many thousands of light years ago. This is all in your now.

And now, so what? What does this mean for you? Well, it will mean something different for each of you. And yet, today we would like to describe a few of the more seemingly impossible things for you to consider. We will lay out a buffet and you can serve yourselves.

There is a threshold of vibration that you are approaching that will allow you to begin choosing new ways of being and experiencing your 'reality'. We place that word in quotes because, as long as you are in a physical environment, you are in what has been termed illusion. That simply means that everything you see is extremely temporary.

It is, or will soon be, possible for you to exercise many abilities that you have not had the experience of before now. If you think that you have these already, be aware that there are still more. Each will begin on the ground where they now stand. That is ever the only way. We ask you to be aware of what is happening around you. There are going to be those who have no idea at all of what they are seeing, or hearing, or beginning to know. They may very likely think they are totally alone and are going crazy. Part of your reason for being where you are is to help these to know that they are beginning to experience the new 'normal'.

Now we will get a bit farther 'out there'. You may find yourselves spending time... let's call that having experience... on more than one earth. The new earth that you have been talking about for quite a while is already a reality. You may find yourselves moving your awareness to that dimension. Notice we did not say 'going there'. No one where you now are focused will likely understand that you are gone. Once there, you will experience an entirely different kind of life. That is, after all, what you have been working toward. You may choose to bring back to your current focus much that you learn there in order to help those that remain. They will experience a totally 'new you', but will not know anything else. It may even take you a while to understand, and that is part of the reason for our telling you this. Sort of a teaser, you might say. At first, it may seem as though you are having very realistic dreams that are rather far out. Enjoy. It will get better.

What you experience, and what you choose or do not choose, will be entirely up to you. That has always been the case, even though the veil has kept you from understanding it. What we would like you to be aware of, at this time, is that you will not choose anything that will leave anyone behind. To the contrary, the farther ahead you choose to venture, the greater your positive effect for those who follow. You are truly multidimensional. It is your awareness of that fact that will grow. You will not leave anyone behind.

Now, we know that these things may be a bit of a stretch for you, and that is OK. But perhaps it may be fun to let your imaginations stretch and allow yourselves to consider what this may mean. For instance, might it mean that you have reached a point that allows your greater being the freedom to inhabit more of your physical existence? Go with that, if you like. None of you have any clear idea of what approaches anyway, so let your minds reach out and play. Have fun. It's about time, don't you think?

As usual, we close by saying that we are with you, we support you, and we love you. Ask for help when you need it. Good day.

It is now a bit of time since the super moon and the equinox that was said to be many things. Congratulations. You've made it. Somehow it seems as if the world did not come to an end. And somehow, even though you do not seem to be able to put your finger on it, you feel that something is different. Well, you are correct, it is. And if you allow us, we will put our finger on it for you.

What has happened is that you have entered yet another area of higher frequency and it is affecting you and helping you to raise your own vibration and become even more of the highest possible being that you can become. This has actually been going on for some time. This universe operates in cycles and waves, as you know. And you have simply moved onto a higher plateau, if you will.

Now, if we may, let us suggest that you explore once again, or continue to explore, who you are. What do you love? What gives you joy? We ask you to do this because you will increasingly find now that these will be the things that you seem to be gifted in. Some people are already stunned at finding skills they did not even realize they had. You have lived many lives there, you know. And you have honed a great many skills, developed many talents. Think of it as a toolbox that you now may draw from. And we advise you, that perhaps the best way to go about this is to look for ways that you can be helpful where you are and then see how you feel about that. When you get that "Gee, it would be neat if I could..." feeling, try that. You just may surprise yourself. Now, you may experience this as a giant step forward in something that you already do. That, of course, is just fine. You may find your life taking an about-face. If that feels good to you, flow with it. But do not let yourself be dragged into things that do not please you. Your feelings are a guidance system that you brought to where you are for a reason. They are intended to help you. Use them.

Think of these new energies as a springboard. Take a couple of bounces and then fly. Where are you guided by your feelings to go? Ask us to show you, if you do not see. But then be prepared to step forward into the situations that arise. Too often you have second-guessed what has been provided. Go with the flow means go with the flow. It does not mean figure out where you are going. It means that you are ready to allow your own higher knowing, that sees around corners and over hills where you do not, to guide you. And the guidance, until you can hear it, will come in feelings and synchronicities. You will notice those increasing. That is the communication between us becoming clearer. There will be a breakthrough. Be patient with yourself.

Now, having spoken of cycles and waves, let us say that these have not only not come to an end but will continue to increase in both intensity and frequency of occurrence. We have always moderated these for you personally so that you are not overwhelmed. We shall continue to do so. But understand that your Higher Self has an agenda also. So at times you find a wee bit of stress here and there. How might you deal with it? As always, we advise that you throw open your arms and accept what you have invited with gratitude. You will always find that this will keep any discomfort to a minimum.

It is time to think about living in your new world. You are building it. As we said at the beginning, congratulations!

We would speak with you today regarding the emotional load you have attached to the events you imagine, yes we said imagine, during the final weeks of this month.

There are so many things, both beneficial and worrisome for you, which have been forecast for this time, that it would be a lengthy discussion just to list them all. There are those focused on financial benefit or fear of great loss. There are those who are certain that a great reconstruction of your governments is on its way. There are those that fear a cosmic event that will demolish most of your earth. There are those that believe thousands of craft from other worlds will at long last arrive, and much more. We said it would be a long list.

As gently and lovingly as we can, let us point out to you that you are missing the point, just as you did at the end of 2012. Remember the many expectations that you had attached to that time? Remember the disappointment that everyone felt when those things did not happen as anticipated? You are setting yourselves up for just such a disappointment again.

In 2012, there was an almost universal cry of "Nothing happened!" That was because you had almost completely missed the point of what you had felt coming by interpreting the subconscious knowing as the message that all of the things you most dearly wished for were going to be delivered to you from some outside source or other. Let us state once again for you the reality of what is occurring.

We, on this side of the 'veil', and that includes the far greater portion of yourselves than you are aware of, serve as the architects, mentors, and guides of the illusory 'reality' that you are using to learn lessons from. How you got into this state and why is an entirely different discussion. What is important for this message is that the 'reality', that results from all of these current energies and the changes that they are bringing about, will be built by you as a reflection of you. So in order to enjoy this time and not be emotionally flattened by it, we would have you change your focus.

Some things that you envision may actually take place over time. That is true. It is also true that many may not. In order to see the things you actually want to see, you must place your desire, intent, and focus on those things and not on their opposites. And that is still not the core of this message.

We have stressed to you over and again that the most important thing that is happening, at this time, is that you yourselves are changing. Your physical makeup is changing. Your mental life is changing. And your spiritual being is becoming more and more able to incorporate itself into your physical existence, as a result. This is the most important thing that is happening on your planet at this time, indeed at any time, in her history.

Nothing concerning any of those other things we mentioned above could happen without this. They, if and when they occur, will happen only as a result of these changes we stress to you. Any other expectations you may have, as an individual, will be missing the point in a very important way. Remember when you read that you should "Render unto Caesar the things which are Caesar's?" That is something that you must yet learn how to do.

To take liberties with a common quote, you are not physical beings playing with spiritual things. You are spiritual beings playing with very temporary, illusory, and relatively unimportant things. We know, that because of your focus, they seem to be extremely important. But that is the point, you see. You are giving them a power that they do not inherently possess. And the source of the power that you give them is yourselves.

Now let us say this. Yes, these are very important times. Yes, immense change is occurring. Yes, that can mean for each of you, as well. But the benefit can be far greater if you place your focus where it is most beneficial to place it. Throw your arms open wide and accept, with deep gratitude, the very personal and applicable changes that are available to each of you at this time. We promise you that this will not be disappointing. All around you, those who understand this are advancing on their own spiritual journeys. We invite you to join them.

Much is being thrown at you in order to distract you. Know this for what it is, and you will find yourselves actually living in a different world. Read that how you wish. We will end this here with our dearest hope that you will contemplate these words closely. Good day.

It Rings True

.

Miscellaneous

Safety

We choose today to speak about the subject of safety. And so, naturally, we shall begin by taking a look at fear.

Fear is one of your biggest obstacles. For many it is a constant companion. It is, in the final analysis, a lack of faith in oneself, in one's future, and a lack of understanding and faith in the Universe itself. Have you not heard throughout your life that your life itself is eternal? No matter where you are, no matter what your faith, even if you think you have no faith, this is something that is a deep part of your being.

The knowing of this deeply within your consciousness is the reason that it is pervasive in all of your world's religions. And yet you fear.

Of course, no one enjoys physical pain. No one enjoys suffering. Everyone wishes to have abundance, joy, freedom. No one wishes to lose these when they experience them. The fear we are speaking of is your ultimate fear. You fear death. You say that you believe there is no death, yet you fear death.

Now, it is true that the body's mind has a fear reaction to pain and wishes to live, even in its last instant. And it is also true that by far the greatest number of you identify with the body that you inhabit. Even if you have studied and believed great numbers of teachings that say you are not that body, still you identify with it. You feel as if you are inside of that body and that you are not outside of it. For what it may be worth, we tell you that you are outside of it and that it is inside of you.

But we are speaking of safety, of security. How can you find this?

Instead of living in a constant feeling of being in peril of losing your life, what if you could live in constant knowing that nothing could possibly take that life from you? Would thinking it work? Not really. Professing it? You do that. Does it work? Not really. Blind faith? Doesn't seem to work so well, does it? What produces real trust is experience. Does that seem true? This is, in fact, why those who have had what you call near death experiences are forever changed.

So let's all run out and have one of those. Please do not try this at home.

Now if you could experience the memories of having lived several times before, if you could experience the memory of being outside of your body and still being here to tell about it, would that help? Of course it would. Isn't that a great part of what happens to those you call adepts in many of what you call spiritual practices?

And once one experiences these things, a great load is lifted from them. Now they know, you see, that they are not their body. They know that they live with or without it. It is only a creation that allows physical experiences. And they begin to learn that their total experience is far more than physical.

As earth humans have progressed recently, there have been many methods of reaching these memories and experiences that have become quite popular. Still, however, it cannot be said that anything like a majority of you are on that path... yet. But we tell you that will change along with everything else. Your memories are returning.

And along with the memories will come that knowing, that certainty, that you are eternal, that this moment is the only time that is. And that is security. That is safety.

We trust we have given you food for thought. Be at peace. Good day.

Gratitude

Today is the day that the country of our channel has labeled Thanksgiving. We know that giving thanks is the daily, even constant, practice of many of those who read and listen to our messages. And we further know that those of you who do this need no reminder of the immense power of this consciousness of gratitude in your lives. We wish, however, to recommend it to any who are beginning on what you term 'the path'.

It has been said that if one had only one prayer, and that one were "thank you", it would be all one ever needed. We affirm that to be very true, indeed. As affirmation of this, we ask you to put yourself in the place of the one being thanked. Imagine how you would feel. Would you not then do all you could for the one being so considerate as to thank you for what you had done?

Now, while it is true that your Creator, as well as those of us you call guides, angels, masters and so on, will never cease in our efforts in your behalf, we do very much appreciate your acknowledgment of those efforts. And if it is possible to imagine us redoubling the light, love, and help we send to you, then be assured we do just that.

On this day you call Thanksgiving, we also offer gratitude. We offer gratitude to the Divine for our opportunity to serve. And we offer our deepest gratitude and appreciation for those beings who are immersed, due to their own desire to be of service to the ALL, in the evolution of consciousness on your planet. We speak of you. We are in accord with your journey and will continue to aid you in every way open to us. May your efforts for others and for yourselves bring results even far surpassing your imaginations.

May the blessings and light of the Divine be yours this day.

Discernment

We return this day to speak with you regarding the shift that you now recognize as an ongoing part of your beings. You have, for some time, been aware that changes are now a part of your inner life. Everything, actually, is changing for you, just as you have expressed the desire for. This gives us a wide choice of what to discuss. We choose your knowing, or a part thereof.

We wish to speak of your ability to know whether what you are hearing, reading, or seeing is truth. Does it, or does it not, agree with what your Highest Self knows to be true? You call this resonating. In other words, you say that it vibrates at a frequency that harmonizes with your own—a very apt description.

Now, when you are seeking to make these determinations, be aware that you require to 'be' in your heart space and not in your intellect, in what you somewhat mistakenly call your mind. Your mind, you see, is far greater than the intellect. When you assess the resonance of what you are in perception of from your heart, you are weighing it against vast stores of knowledge that your intellect, at least so far, is unaware of. The feelings that are invoked will give you a true indication of whether or not this 'resonates' with you. There is still, however, one sticky little problem, one which you are learning to navigate past.

When you have learned to believe things that seem to contradict what your heart is saying, you still often tend to choose what your intellect is telling you. You choose 'knowledge' over wisdom. We know that we seem to be speaking of something that contradicts your current definitions of wisdom. But what we are doing actually is teaching you to expand your definitions. We are saying that what you access when you look into your heart for answers is much greater and more reliable than anything you have been taught about yourselves.

There are many, many teachings these days concerning that of which we speak. These are not new. The teachings of love and wisdom have been around for a long, long time. But it has come about that you have reached a point where mankind, as a whole, and not just a few dedicated adepts, is now able to assimilate these concepts into their lives. And so the careful nurturing of these ideas in hidden places has evolved into a full-fledged effort to spread them far and wide.

Still, you are, if you are reading this close to the time it is being given, on the cutting edge, so to speak. You are being reminded of things which you have known forever. You were asked to forget. Now you are being prompted to remember. We will discuss others of these things as times progress.

We said that there were things changing in your inner life. This will continue, and at the end of the next year, you will be less like you are today than you now are like the you of a year ago. Approach this like an adventure to be enjoyed and anticipated, and it need not be uncomfortable for you. We even urge you to imagine what it might be like, but do not limit it. You might want to add "or something better" to your daydreams.

Remember to connect with us daily through your feelings. When you 'search' for us in this manner, you will quickly learn to know of our presence. This, too, is enhanced from your previous state. It was always true, but now you vibrate higher. You are learning to catch up with the changes you now embody. Look around you for those whom you know are holding this higher energy, and spend time with them. It rubs off. (If you see us grinning, you are correct.) Good day.

Abundance/Response Ability

We understand that this day is the beginning of a new cycle in your method of counting. We wish you a cycle of great transformation and joy in your abundance. Concerning your abundance, we would wish you to consider the following:

You are abundant. There is no one incarnate upon your planet who is not living in abundance. There is no lack. You create everything you see. The obvious question, if you accept that, is what am I creating and why. Why am I creating, if I am indeed so very powerful, things which I do not prefer?

There are many possible answers to that question. But there will be no answers to it until the question is finally asked. Do you see? One cannot see how and why one is doing something as long as one believes the responsibility (response ability) lies elsewhere. Notice, please that we did NOT use or mention the word blame. And that is why it is taught so often that one needs to take complete responsibility for everything is one's life. When that is assumed, claimed for oneself, then the power of response ability returns to where it belongs. And so we wish for you this in your new year. May you turn your wishes for the upcoming twelve months into intentions. May you feel the joy of what the fulfillment of those intentions will bring. May you maintain your focus until those visions become your reality. And finally, may you take from that the lesson of how very powerful you truly are.

May the abundance of the universe that constantly surrounds you miraculously become that which you prefer.

Positivity

You have made your plans. You have reservations. You have tickets. You have your route all laid out. You have your agenda written. And suddenly, something happens that makes it apparent that things are not going to go exactly as you expected. How do you react to that? Most of you immediately go into the oh-no-this-is-terrible mode. You allow your imagination to fly off into the seeing of the worst of possibilities. This you have honed to a fine degree of expertise through many years, if not many lifetimes. It is such a universal response in your environment that no one even notices. What do you suppose that brings to you? And why do you suppose that it might have happened? That is, in fact, the universally asked question. "Why?"

Well, although many of you will still have trouble with this concept, we will tell you that it is an opportunity either to offer you something better or to prevent something worse. We have told you often that we work with you always to bring you what is in your highest and best interest. Too many do not know that or have not yet begun to operate as if it is truly the case.

If it is the latter case that we are giving you the opportunity to avoid something you do not, on your level of conscious awareness, foresee, then you may not become aware of what that might have been. Yet maybe, it will become apparent. Perhaps there will be a report that your planned route, flight, or destination had a problem that you were spared. You have all heard those stories.

If it is, indeed, the case that something even better than you have planned might be offered, what do you suppose will happen when you go into the negative, shutting down, oh no mindset? We do not believe it necessary to elaborate. You all know of the Law of Attraction. You are all aware that you bring more of whatever you are feeling. And almost all of you are at least beginning to train yourselves to keep your energy higher in frequency as much as you can.

Now we are not suggesting that you begin a struggle to learn not to go into the 'oh-no' mode. We are going to suggest that you learn another way and just let that old pattern wither and drop off. Doesn't that seem easier? Some of you already do this, and to you we say "Bravo". It is really very simple, and when we suggest it, all you need to do is try it a few times. At the very least, it will save you some coins through the non-purchase of antacids. But we assure you that it is as powerful as it is simple. It opens the way for us to help you manifest that better thing instead of closing the chances down.

We are making this long and verbose explanation in order that you understand this well instead of dismissing it. It truly is simple. But most really powerful things are. Here we go.

Next time something like this occurs for you, try this out. As soon as you catch yourself going into the 'oh-no' mode, think this: "I wonder what wonderful thing is in store for me that is even better!" Then let your imagination take off in the other direction. Allow your anticipation to build. Even become excited, if you like. Can you feel how your energy would rise? Can you see how the result of that upsurge of positivity will be only beneficial? Try it. You'll like it.

Value

Today we will speak of value. This is not a subject we have addressed here before, but we feel that at this time it may be well to do so.

What is value? How may it be best determined? Is it being determined in the best way today? Let us suggest today that perhaps the understanding of what value is may need to be modified somewhat.

The true measure of value is whether a thing, a thought, or an action is beneficial to life. The ultimate value to a being, to your being, is life itself. Does the thing being valued enhance life? Does it harm life? That is always at the heart of your own determinations, is it not? Perhaps you might be mistaken, but do you not always determine your valuation of something by what you perceive to be best for yourself?

We would suggest, however, that Life be capitalized and be thought of as the one and only universal thing. And then it would be obvious we think that true value would be what is best for the enhancement of all life. Now, you may not feel as though you are the best judge of what is best for all life. And that may very well be true. However, you are hard-wired to do what is best, in your understanding, for yourself. So you may use that measuring stick and apply it to those things that are not personal to you.

That is exactly the basis for what you call The Golden Rule. If it is not the best for me, then I will not do it to another. If it would not benefit my life, I will not do it. Period.

Ah, but what if one is short-sighted? What if one is only concerned with one's own immediate gratification? That is precisely the major problem on your world today, is it not? And we suggest then, that the remedy is for you, as a species, to make the simple change from self-gratification to concern for Life itself. What is best for all? What will be best over the long term? How can I, how can we, improve the quality of Life? That would quite likely be different from the answer to "How can I have more?" And that is why you do understand that those who think and act in that higher way deserve to be held in greater respect.

These are not ideas that are unknown to you. They are not secrets. They are things that your world has, for far too long, chosen to ignore. And that disregard for the consequences to others, to Life itself, has led you to your present situation. Whether one chooses to see it or not, your world is on the precipice of the collapse you have been warned of for many decades. We think that perhaps it is time for your societies to re-think where they are going.

Now, lest this message get too dark, let us say that we see your world waking up to these things in many, many ways and in a great many places. You are not being told of this, because it is not yet perceived that good news 'sells'. But that, too, will change in time.

The value, the benefit to Life, of love, of caring, of helping, of lifting others, other beings, of Life itself is being recognized and spread everywhere. This is beginning to be seen and felt. The calamities that happen in places far away are bringing humanity to humanity. That is a cute turn of phrase, is it not?

You are learning to value the quality of life that other beings have as much as you value your own. You are learning to come together for the benefit of all. And when your environment threatens you, you are beginning to even consider your environment. It's funny how that works. You may even begin to outnumber those who refuse to think in these new ways. It could happen. It is happening.

This is and will continue to be the effect of your expansion of consciousness. It is also one of the main reasons for the need to expand your consciousness. And it is the reason for us always telling you to learn to live from your heart. That is living in empathy and compassion, you see. That is concern for Life. That is value. That is the true measure.

And when one of you begins to live in this way, it has effects upon the mind and the body. The entire life will be transformed. The energy in which you find yourselves now is enhancing this as never before.

We have spoken of this repeatedly in recent messages. The energy signature of your planet is being raised by you and is raising yours, as well. There is contributing energy being applied from outside, also, in every way that is possible. It is decided that your world will change. You, know it or not, have decided to change it. You, know it or not, have decided to change. And we continue to support you in every way possible. Consider this Council as the planning committee and yourselves as the boots-on-the-ground. That is how it works. And that is the only way it will work.

A savior has been sent. Tag, you're it. Now, we know that seems to be the hard way. You really would like to have overwhelming outside help. But the point, you see, is for you to learn and grow, for Life to learn and grow. And you did, you are, and you will... marvelously. If it helps you to understand, then know that this is always the way, everywhere. You are not selected to be the only ones to do this. You are just the current ones, the local ones. Congratulations.

Ascension

We have been speaking to you as The Council for quite some time now. Many of you are fully and personally aware of whom we are. You have had dreams, visions or meditations in which you have met with us. When you hear or read of the council chamber, boardroom, amphitheater, or other setting, you know immediately what is being discussed. And yet we know that quite a few still have questions regarding who and what we are. Today we shall take a slight detour from our usual message and explain this for you.

The Council, as we term it here, is an assembly of those you variously term light beings, angels, guides, teachers, and other aspects of your selves who are in session to help you make decisions regarding your current incarnate lives. There is no one on your world, or any other, who does not have a council. There is no one who does not have access to his or her council. Your own Higher Self has a seat on your council. This should not be surprising, since the council sits for your benefit. This is where your intuition comes from. This is the origin of the hunches, the nudges, the knowing.

When you sleep or meditate, you often come to your council for information and guidance. You will never find that the council is not in session, and there is no information that you might ever need that is not available to you. Often, there is information that is seen to have the potential to disturb your conscious mind that you do not remember upon awakening. That does not mean that you were not given the information and did not make use of it. There is, after all, quite a bit that your Self is aware of and your conscious mind is not... yet. But you will find, as your new year progresses, that many of you become more and more able to embody much more of what you call your Higher Selves.

This development is not new. It has been going on for some time. Many of you have become personally aware of this. You call it ascension. And as your body becomes more able to take on more of your being, you experience varying things that you call ascension symptoms. These are temporary, and we would have you think of them as signposts of progress and not something to be wary of.

Now that you know who we are, we will revert to our normal theme in future messages. You will find that in this year, the messages you receive will flow more and more into this theme from all sources. That is due to the time. It is time for you to finally become aware of whom you are. It is time for you to embody, intentionally and consciously, more of the Divine Selves that you are. Ascension accelerates now. And so, since that is our purpose at this time, you will find that we speak of it often, if not always.

Enjoy the ride!

We will address, at this time, the more widespread experiencing of what you would term ascension symptoms.

Now, it appears to some as if any ache or pain that you have, if you call yourself a lightworker, can be called an ascension symptom. That is almost true, but true in the sense that a headache can be indicative of quite a wide variety of ailments.

What you are going through now, if you are, indeed, in this 'wave' of those who are preparing their bodies for what is to come, is an increasing of the body's ability to hold and use the energies, the light. Part of this is the rising of the body's energy called the kundalini. Part of this is actually the experience of physical changes necessary in the body itself. This can be rather uncomfortable, even painful.

If this is, indeed, what you are experiencing, we wish you to know that you are not going crazy, nor are you about to transition. We, in no way, wish you to interpret this as us telling you not to consult with your physicians. There are still going to be actual needs for medical treatment for other causes, and we do not want you to deny your body's treatment where it is needed.

Know, however, that some of what you experience now may feel so intense that it might cause you to go into panic if you do not understand it. Before you panic, please attempt to ascertain the cause. Perhaps you will wish to read up on the types of things that we are talking about so that you are more prepared and less likely to go into fear around things that are actually happening for your benefit.

As a sub-text to this message, let us point out that you may take these occurrences as indications that you now have real evidence that something is happening. It has amazed us how so many have been able to deny this in the past. To us, it has seemed undeniable. Something is happening. It is happening now. Know this.

Let us say one more thing, however. If you have not noticed anything like we are speaking of, do not judge yourself as lacking. No two of you are the same. No two of you will experience the same things, although you may have many similarities. Can you see yourself saying, "He is in pain. I want to be in pain, too!" We thought not. Just accept, in gratitude, what is your life in this moment. You are what you are, and that is perfect for the moment.

We honor who you are. Do no less for yourselves and those around you.

To continue from where we left off in our last message, we will speak to the subject of what you are calling ascension. We offer, as we have before through this channel and others, that it might be more properly called descension. In other words, you are not becoming your Higher Selves so much as your Higher Selves are preparing you to be able to handle it as they incarnate more of themselves into you. With apologies to Dr. Seuss again, you will become you-er than you.

Much of the discomfort that you have been experiencing is due to the fact that your physical being simply could not have survived this in the state that it was just a short time ago. You have no understanding of the effect that the taking on of such frequency would have had on you. Even now, you will have some rather challenging times ahead, although we shall be as careful as we can not to overload your nervous systems.

We often hear you say, "Bring it on" or "I'm ready". Let us say that there are those who are experiencing the beginnings of their increased consciousness and its effect upon them and are having a bit of a struggle at times, hoping they are not going crazy. We can almost promise you that there are those around you now who dare not tell you some of what they are dealing with. We tell you this, not so that you will be wary of what awaits you, but so that you will be prepared for possibilities that you have not considered or have no frame of reference for.

These things really are, in the context of what we are talking about, not important, other than to have you be a bit prepared. What is important is that you come to understand, and finally to know, that you are, indeed, the very embodiment of the divine being that is the spark of the One that is also at one with the light of your Source.

Now, we hear thoughts and feelings of "that is not new", and "I already know that". Understand that your intellect is talking. When we say know, we mean it as in "I know I am alive." Do you feel, when you say that, how different it is from intellectual understanding?

This is where you are heading. This is what this time is all about. Some of you will go one way to get there, and others will go other ways. That is as it should be. There is no reason, nor is it even desirable, for everyone to ride the same bus. You exist so that The One can experience all of it.

As we said before, enjoy the ride.

More than one hundred years ago, a handful of men, physicists, made discoveries and advanced theories that turned their view of reality on its ear. Now, after all this time, many of those ideas have percolated through your societies far enough to be accepted and at least partially understood by a majority of you.

What has happened in the intervening years is that far, far more has been discovered. There are things that have been discovered, theorized, and proven, even put into use, which are still known to very few of you. And the intent of those who are using these things is that it should stay that way.

The effect of spreading and acceptance of many of these things would revolutionize your entire world. You are being 'protected' from these things.

A great deal of what is known and what is done upon your planet is kept secret. But your understanding of the possibility of that, of secrecy, will be undergoing a bit of change in the near future. As you understand the nature of the oneness of your consciousness, you will come to know that what is known, is known. There is nothing known that you are unable to know. Further, you have been lead to believe that there is much that you would not understand, and you are soon to reach a state of being in which you are able to understand whatever you need and wish to understand.

Now we do not say that you who just read that last line will become all knowing on the day after tomorrow. But surely, as a collective, you are now aware of the expansion that is occurring within you. If you accept these possibilities and wish to participate in this evolution, we ask you to simply open yourself to the possibility that you can and are growing now into a much grander version of yourselves than you have ever dreamed of. And then, in the depth of your being, you may wish to sing out a resounding "YES!"

Proceed upon your forward path now, not as seven billion individuals, but as one family. He is not your brother. She is not your sister. At the truest level, they are you. Learn this well, and your world will never be the same again. You are this close... this close.

About the Author

Ron spent 12 years in the U.S. Air Force, returning to civilian life in 1970. He entered a career in business after leaving the military, which eventually found him managing the purchasing operations for several retail and wholesale companies. He was instrumental in revising the computer use of those companies to include their purchasing functions. After retiring in 2006, he is at last, able to devote much more time to inner work, studying energy healing and opening up to the greater possibilities that have resulted in the of this material. You will find his work on

http://ronahead.wordpress.com

and on Facebook's Oracles and Healers page.

Made in the USA
Middletown, DE
16 June 2019